The Quest Through the Centuries

The Quest
Through the
Centuries

THE SEARCH FOR THE HISTORICAL JESUS

Harvey K. McArthur

Fortress Press   *Philadelphia*

© 1966 Fortress Press

Library of Congress Catalog Card Number 66–14243

2661K65   Printed in the U. S. A.   UB24

To the Students and Faculty

of

North Park College and Seminary

Table of Contents

Introduction

The Quest for the historical Jesus has produced an immense body of literature. Since the bulk of this literature appeared during the past two centuries it is clear that the Quest has been a particular concern of the modern period in the life of the church. Yet, in some sense, the Quest has always been a concern of the church, since the faith of the church has always had its starting point and focus in Jesus of Nazareth. What forms, then, did the Quest take before the rise of modern historiography in the eighteenth and nineteenth centuries? This question guided my work during a sabbatical for the academic year 1961–62, a sabbatical which was spent in Heidelberg, Germany, through the assistance of a Fulbright Research Fellowship. During that time only a few facets of this question could be examined. Therefore this study is not a detailed history of the Quest through the centuries but an attempt to illustrate that Quest by examining the forms it took in selected periods of the church's history. If it were appropriate to use the style of the eighteenth century today the title would have been: *Glimpses into the Quest for the Historical Jesus throughout Christian History, with Special Reference to the Earliest and Latest Periods, and with Reflections on the Inevitability of that Quest, Plus the Author's own Convictions concerning the Present State of the Discussion.*

The opening chapter suggests that the fusion of history and interpretation characteristic of the biblical record and of the Christian faith created a situation in which the Quest for the historical Jesus was inevitable, at least as a minor motif throughout all the church's life. Chapters two to five deal with forms of the Quest in various epochs of the church's history, including the most recent epoch when the question of history became a dominant interest of Western culture, with the result that what had always been a minor motif moved into the center of New Testament studies. Chapter six is an attempt to evaluate the present situation and to indicate my own reactions.

Chapters one, two, five, and six are the substance of the Nils W. Lund Memorial Lectures in Biblical Studies which I had the privilege of giving in November, 1962, at the North Park College and Theological Seminary in Chicago. The revision which these lectures have undergone since their initial presentation has been most extensive in chapter six, which deals with crucial contemporary issues. A slightly condensed version of chapter four was read at the annual meeting of the Society of Biblical Literature in December, 1962.

It is with some hesitation that I commit to the indelibility of print the views expressed in chapter six. We stand in the midst of the discussion, and there is a temptation to postpone commitment to any one position until the issues have received further clarification. My hesitation has been overcome, first, by the fact that my acceptance of the invitation to give the Nils W. Lund Lectures included the responsibility of publication, and, second, by the conviction that the issues can be clarified only as those concerned with them express their views in order to stimulate debate and correction. While my own views have been expressed in the closing pages, I have been more concerned to describe the options which confront us as we consider the relation between the Jesus of history and the Christ of faith. I have not hidden my suspicion that some scholars have attempted to evade the questions underlined by Professor Bultmann's form criticism by insisting that we "know" more about the historical Jesus than Bultmann has been willing to concede. But all knowledge derived from historical research is probability knowledge, i.e., it may be more or less probable, but it is never certain in any absolute sense. The radical character of Bultmann's position has served to emphasize this hard fact. The central issue is how the certainties of faith are to be related to the uncertainties of research. This issue is not resolved simply by being a little more conservative than Professor Bultmann. Whether the suggestions in chapter six are any more helpful in the resolution of this problem must be left to the judgment of the readers. It is a pleasure to express once again to President Karl H. Olsson and Dean Donald C. Frisk my appreciation for the cordial reception I received from them and their colleagues at North Park.

HARVEY K. MCARTHUR

1

The Inevitability
of the
Quest

In 1910 Albert Schweitzer's book *Von Reimarus zu Wrede* was published in English with the title *The Quest of the Historical Jesus*. Because of its encyclopedic character the book has been read in its entirety by comparatively few, but the title was an immediate and continuing success. It was a success because it summed up in a single phrase the most important aspect of New Testament studies in the modern period, i.e., the period since the late eighteenth century. The Quest was an attempt to reconstruct the ministry of Jesus with an understanding of its inner and outer development. It presupposed a greater or lesser degree of contrast between the words and acts of Jesus during his earthly ministry and the theological portrait which emerged during the succeeding generations. The term "Quest" rightly suggests that the leaders of this movement assumed that their proposed reconstruction was a formidable task and one which could not be accomplished simply by pasting portions of the Gospels together.

More than half a century has passed since the publication of Schweitzer's book. During this period it has sometimes seemed as if the English title would serve not only as a description but also as an epitaph for the movement described. Responsible voices have suggested that the Quest is historically impossible as well as theologically unnecessary and perhaps actually dangerous. This reversal of front in New Testament scholarship has created confusion, at least in the minds of those who read the books reflecting modern research, and possibly even in the minds of those who write such books. It would be presumptuous for any scholar to imagine that he occupies some Olympian mount from which this confusion may be objectively surveyed and the true directions indicated. However, each scholar has an obligation to grapple with the problem and to contribute his widow's mite to the discussion with the hope that the accumulation of such contributions may lead to something substantial.

This first chapter is concerned with the inevitability of the Quest, i.e., with the factors in the biblical tradition itself which made inevitable a tension between the Jesus of history and the Christ of faith.[1] Whenever the church has become conscious of this tension it has been compelled to grapple, in one way or another, with the problem of the historical Jesus. It is understandable that the awareness of this tension has been most acute in periods when the church has been in intellectual conflict with the surrounding culture. In this respect the two outstanding periods have been the early centuries, when the church was compelled to formulate its faith over against the culture of the Greco-Roman world, and the modern period, when the Renaissance inheritance necessitated a rethinking and reformulation of that faith. The intensity of the modern Quest is related to the preoccupation of modern culture with the whole question of history and its meaning. Nevertheless, all periods show some trace of this tension between the historical and the theological elements in the Christian faith, because this tension is implicit in the faith itself.

---

[1] For the present purpose the phrase "Jesus of history" means Jesus as he would have been described by a secular historian had such a person been present in first-century Palestine. It is this "Jesus of history" whom the modern, secular historian is able to recapture partially and with varying degrees of probability. On the other hand, the "Christ of faith" is that same historical figure as described or defined by the professional or popular theology of the church.

I

We may begin with the widely accepted affirmation: *biblical religion is historical religion.* This does not mean simply that biblical religion has a history. Every religion which lasts long enough to become the object of discussion has a history. This affirmation means that in biblical religion God is known through the encounter with historical events. History is medium for revelation. The historical event of the exodus, hidden though its details may be to the historian, is the event which has forever colored the national consciousness of Israel. "I am the Lord your God, who brought you out of the land of Egypt" (Exod. 20:2). The significance of the statement that biblical religion is historical religion becomes clearer when other types of religion are considered. Thus nature religion, unlike historical religion, is religion in which God is understood to be revealed through the processes of nature. The fertility cults of the ancient East, against which Israel struggled, represented nature religion with its preoccupation with the cycle of birth, life, and death both in nature and in mankind. On Easter, with its parades and eggs and bunnies, one sometimes wonders whether Elijah and Elisha lived in vain, since nature religion seems on the point of triumphing over the religion of historical event. Again, philosophical religion is religion created by the thinker in his study. It is a religion of abstract propositions hammered together by the logic of the philosopher's mind and then projected onto the world as a whole. Mystical religion is the religion of the individual mystic who projects himself, or his spirit, out of the visible world of space and sense into the infinite, where he experiences an encounter with that which he regards as transcending all times and all places.

In its totality biblical religion contains elements which reflect these various types of religious experience; but at its center it is historical religion, i.e., the faith which emerged from Israel's encounter with its history in the exodus, in the days of the judges, in the united and divided monarchies, and in the days of the

exile and the disappointing return. In its own way the Christian
community is the inheritor of this entire tradition. For the Christian community, however, this inheritance has been transformed
by the faith which emerged through the encounter with the historical person, Jesus of Nazareth, who lived, taught, worked wonders, died, and was seen again. We who call ourselves Christian
are those who find the center of life and of meaning in the
circle of events connected with this historical person, proclaimed
to us as the Christ, the Son of man, the Son of God, the Lord of
life—Lord of our life and that of the entire world.

Every form of religious experience or tradition has its own
distinctive problems when submitted to the analysis of man's
limited powers of understanding. Historical religion is no exception to this truth. In order to understand the central problems connected with historical religion it is necessary to distinguish, though certainly not to separate, history, kerygma, and
record. Many of us have been conditioned by a theology which,
to describe the entire process of revelation, speaks of "event"
with a capital "E." If we are to use the term "Event" in this
fashion, then we must distinguish between the historical Event,
the kerygmatic Event, and the recorded Event. Or, to put it differently, we must distinguish between the Event as history, the
Event as kerygma, and the Event as record. To simplify the
phraseology the single words history, kerygma, and record will
be used.

For the purpose of this study these terms will carry the following meanings. *History* refers to the literal, external happenings
in and through which the believing community encountered God,
e.g., the exodus from Egypt, or the life and ministry of Jesus.
In this sense history may be thought of as a series of external
events which could have been recorded by a ninteenth-century
historiographer had he lived early enough.

Kerygma refers to the significance, the meaning, the revelation,
which came to the believing community through its participation

in the history or through its remembering of that history. Presumably it is unnecessary to point out that kerygma is simply the anglicizing of a Greek term meaning "that which was proclaimed." In the present context it means "that which was proclaimed by the history to the believing community." If more subtle theological distinctions were necessary it might be proper to distinguish between "that which was proclaimed by the history" and "that which was heard by the community." The former phraseology stresses the objective "proclaiming," while the latter lays emphasis on the subjective "hearing." For our present purposes this distinction may be ignored, since the central question is not affected by the choice of expression used.

Record refers to the results of the attempt by the believing community to perpetuate the history and the kerygma by retelling the story of their experience. Presumably the record was originally oral, but in the process of time it was written down. For our purposes it may be identified with the Bible or with that portion of the Bible relevant to the particular bit of history or kerygma under consideration.

Thus we have *history, kerygma,* and *record.* I do not claim any remarkable originality in the selection of these terms, or any magical efficacy in their use. In some ways they are not fully satisfactory, but at least they will serve as a form of shorthand, as substitutes for whole paragraphs which otherwise would need to be repeated all too frequently.

What is the relationship between the history that occurred, the kerygma that was experienced, and the record that ensued? It is immediately clear that the record was an attempt to reflect history and kerygma in combination. Israel did not repeat the story of the exodus to provide source materials for doctoral theses on happenings around the Red Sea—or was it the Sea of Reeds?—about the year 1300 B.C. They repeated the story so as to give substance to the basic affirmation of their faith, "I am the Lord your God, who brought you out of the land of Egypt. . ." (Exod. 20:2;

Deut. 5:6; *et al.*). Similarly the Christian community did not re-peat the story of Jesus to provide materials for research in com-parative religions, psychic phenomena, Jewish sectarian move-ments, or Hellenistic syncretism. They repeated the old, old story so "that you may believe that Jesus is the Christ, the Son of God, and that believing you may have life in his name" (John 20:31). In both cases what was repeated was a story or narrative and not abstract, theological statements, because the faith of both com-munities had originated in response to actual historical occur-rences. In their record they did not distinguish between history and kerygma, and it is this record with its fusion of history and kerygma which we encounter in our reading of the biblical text. For better or for worse we have learned to distinguish the two, or, more accurately, we have learned to attempt such a distinction. In fact we have been so conditioned by the techniques of recent generations that we tend to ask the record only the question of history, and to assume that if we can get the history straight we can judge the kerygma—or even create it—for ourselves. The result of this emphasis is that when we read the Bible the first question often raised is: Did it really happen that way? This is a legitimate question and one which we learn as children to ask of the stories read to us by our parents. However, since the record is witness to kerygma as well as to history, it would be equally relevant to ask as our opening question: What is the kerygma to which this passage points? In recent years many have learned to begin with this latter question, and they have found this method rewarding, particularly in the study of the Gospels.

II

But let us return to our original question. What is the relation between the record, which we possess, and the history or the kerygma? The most comforting answer would be that the record presents inerrantly both the history and the kerygma. While this answer is comforting, I do not believe it to be the truth. Any discussion of the concept of inspiration, or of the results of inspiration, is bound to lead to controversy, so the subject here under consideration cannot be considered without risking serious differences of opinion. I have stated that I do not believe that the record, i.e., the Bible, presents the history inerrantly. (The question of the kerygma may be set aside until the following section.) Having been brought up in a tradition which took for granted that the record presented inerrant history I am appreciative of this tradition and understand something of its power. But when for the first time I sat down with a Greek harmony of the Gospels and over a period of months worked through that harmony, it ceased to be possible for me to regard the record as inerrant history in the ordinary sense of that term. Every rereading of the Gospel harmony throughout the past twenty-five years has confirmed my initial conclusion. The Gospel writers, or their sources, were simply not concerned with the kind of historical accuracy which we take for granted in the writing of history. The methods of the evangelists were those of a different period and probably of a different purpose. Confusion is increased if twentieth-century historical methodology is made into a procrustean bed for the Gospels. The Gospels must be interpreted in the light of the evangelists' own methods and purposes and not in the light of those which we would employ for a biography or a historical narrative. And the evangelists' methods and purposes did not include accuracy of historical detail.

Mark 5:1–20 will serve as an illustration. This narrative describes the healing of the Gerasene demoniac. Matthew 8:28–34 presents what is almost universally regarded as another version of the same incident. But in Matthew there are two demoniacs, while in Mark (and also in Luke 8:26–39) there is only one. When I was in college a Bible teacher whom I greatly respected, and whom I still respect, attempted to harmonize these two versions of a single incident by saying, "Well, if there were two demoniacs there was also one. Mark mentions only that one, but he does not deny the existence of the second." This is a curious bit of logic. It did not satisfy me then, nor was I wholly convinced that it satisfied my teacher. If that logic were correct, then, by the same logic, there could actually have been three demoniacs with Mark mentioning one of them and Matthew two. For that matter there could have been fifty! So far as I am concerned this is simply a circuitous way of saying that the text is not inerrant. In an earlier day, when it was assumed that the evangelists wrote independently, it could be argued that their general agreement in substance as over against detail was evidence for the historical reliability of the substance which they had in common. Even then the question of inerrancy in detail remained, since the differing details were sometimes discrepant, or apparently discrepant. But this problem is raised even more sharply when it is granted, as is now generally done, that Matthew used Mark as a basic source and, therefore, the minor variations in detail represent the exercise of editorial freedom rather than the use of an independent source. The extent of the problem becomes clearer when we remember that such editorial revision must be assumed to have gone on not merely when the author of Matthew revised Mark but also during the generation that intervened between the events themselves and the Gospel of Mark, the earliest record of Jesus' ministry available to us. We can identify the changes between Mark and Matthew, but we can only speculate concerning those between the original events and Mark. The crucial fact is that the evangelists were not concerned with inerrancy of detail; therefore, there is a gap and a tension between the original history and the record.

A second illustration may be useful even though it is clear that the multiplication of such isolated instances does not prove the case against inerrancy. These illustrations serve merely to suggest the type of evidence which exists in abundance and which must be refuted by the defenders of inerrancy. In Mark 10:35 ff. it is related that James and John came to Jesus asking that in his glory one might sit on his right hand and the other on his left. The same incident is recorded in Matthew 20:20 ff., but in that version the sons of Zebedee are accompanied by their mother, and it is explicitly stated that she was the one who asked the question and who received the initial reply. So far as substance is concerned the difference is not great, but this is a significant illustration of the freedom with which the author of Matthew revised the text of Mark. A modern historian asks: Who did make the request of Jesus? Was it the two sons? Or their mother? Those who assume that Matthew is based on Mark will find it natural to say that this was an editorial revision carried out by Matthew in the interest of preserving the reputations of the two sons of Zebedee. A mother may be excused for being ambitious for her children; she was not one of the pillars of the church, and, anyway, she was only a woman! That Matthew did modify Mark for these or other reasons is confirmed by a trifling detail which is apparent in Greek but not in modern English. Greek distinguishes the singular "you" ("thou" in the KJV) from the plural "you" ("ye" in the KJV). In the parallel presentation of the two versions given below, "you" in the singular is printed in Roman type, while "you" in the plural is printed in italics:

Matthew 20:20 ff.	Mark 10:35 ff.
20 Then the mother of the sons of Zebedee came up to him, with her sons, and kneeling before him she asked for something. 21 And he said to her, "What do you want?"	35 And James and John, the sons of Zebedee, came forward to him, and said to him, "Teacher, we want you to do for us whatever we ask of you." 36 And he said to them, "What do *you* want me to do for *you?*"
She said to him, "Command that these two sons of mine may sit, one at your right hand and one at your left, in your kingdom." 22 But Jesus answered, "*You* do not know what *you* are asking. Are *you* able to drink the cup that I am to drink?"	37 And they said to him, "Grant us to sit, one at your right hand and one at your left, in your glory." 38 But Jesus said to them, "*You* do not know what *you* are asking. Are *you* able to drink the cup that I drink, or to be baptized with the baptism with which I am baptized?" 39 And they said to
They said to him, "We are able."	him, "We are able."

In Mark's version of the story Jesus is addressed by the two sons of Zebedee and in replying to them uses, appropriately, the plural "you" throughout. In the Gospel of Matthew Jesus is addressed by one person, namely, the mother of James and John. In his initial reply to her Jesus is reported to have used the singular "you," but in the continuing conversation the singular disappears and is replaced by the plural found in the Marcan parallel.

If the question of "Scripture" were not involved here, everyone would agree that the author of Matthew revised Mark in order to shift the onus of blame to the mother. At the precise point of the change he remembered to substitute a singular "you" for the natural plural in his Marcan source, but he neglected to revise the conversation throughout. Since Matthew 20:22b–23 is obviously directed to the sons of Zebedee, it would have been difficult for the evangelist to have revised this section in harmony with his representation that the conversation was between Jesus and the mother of James and John. Thus the internal evidence confirms the thesis that Mark was revised by the author of Matthew. The procedure we have followed above in comparing these two passages is a relatively harmless one from the point of view of the central ethical and religious thrust of the passages, but it underlines the difficulties involved in any doctrine of inerrancy.

Many Roman Catholic scholars recognize quite freely that such discrepancies exist between the same narrative in different Gospels. But they continue to speak of "inerrancy" by interpreting that concept to mean that the Scriptures are "inerrant" for the purpose God intended, though they may not be inerrant in the ordinary sense of being historically accurate. Thus a kind of theological inerrancy may be affirmed despite the recognition of numerous errors of fact in the realm of history or science. Recently a Roman Catholic journal presented a thoughtful article with the paradoxical title "Inerrant Errors."[2] It is particularly

[2] H. J. Richards, "Inerrant Errors," *Scripture*, XIV, No. 28 (October, 1962), 97–109.

appropriate to mention Roman Catholic scholars in this context since they cannot so easily be accused of having succumbed to a modernistic or rationalistic rejection of the supernatural in their interpretation of Scripture. While the term "inerrancy" may be retained in this fashion, it is clear that it is no longer the older version of that concept. It is equally clear that this view allows for the tension between the record and the history, and it was the acute awareness of this tension which led, finally, to the modern form of the Quest for the historical Jesus.

It has sometimes been urged that this questioning of the in-errancy of Scripture is suspect because it is a distinctively modern phenomenon. Admittedly, the radical character of much biblical criticism is a modern phenomenon, but it would be a serious mistake to assume that the church throughout the centuries has always accepted the inerrancy of the Bible in matters of fact. The church Fathers had a high doctrine of Scripture, but they did not all deduce from this doctrine that statements of fact were there-fore necessarily correct. Perhaps Origen was the most outspoken in this respect, but he was certainly not alone in his view. Writ-ing early in the third century he was one of the first to deal di-rectly with the historical criticisms raised by those outside the church.[3] A succinct statement of his repudiation of inerrancy is found in Book X, chapter 4, of his *Commentary on John,* where he says of the evangelists:

> I do not condemn them if they even sometimes dealt freely with things which to the eye of history happened differently, and changed them so as to subserve the mystical aims they had in view; so as to speak of a thing which happened in a certain place, as if it had happened in another, or of what took place at a certain time, as if it had taken place at another time, and to introduce into what was spoken in a certain way some changes of their own. They proposed to speak the truth where it was possible both

[3] His treatise *Against Celsus* is an example of such a reply to critics.

materially and spiritually, and where this was not possible it was
their intention to prefer the spiritual to the material. The spiritual
truth was often preserved, as one might say, in the material false-
hood. . . .[4]

Again, the four books of Augustine's *The Harmony of the
Gospels* are devoted to defending the basic accuracy of those
documents against the criticism leveled at them in his day. In
order to carry out this defense Augustine feels obliged to concede quite freely that the evangelists have frequently violated the
chronological order of the actual events, setting them forth "in
accordance with the recollection each retained of them," and that
they have on occasion inserted words of their own in place of,
or in addition to, the original words spoken.[5]

The Reformers stressed the authority of Scripture over against
the authority of the church, but it is well known that Luther dealt
somewhat cavalierly with aspects of biblical teaching and narrative.[6] Calvin, though far more strict in his systematic formulations of the concept of inspiration, was prepared to admit that
the historical statements of the evangelists were not always to
be interpreted with complete literalness. Thus in his *Commentary
on a Harmony of the Evangelists, Matthew, Mark, and Luke* he
insists that the Sermon on the Mount of Matthew 5–7 is a collection of sayings from various occasions, despite the framework
in which it has been placed by the evangelist.[7]

[4] Origen, *Commentary on John*, Bk. X, sec. 4; we cite from the translation by
Allan Menzies in *The Ante-Nicene Fathers*, Vol. IX (New York, 1896; reprinted
but numbered Vol. X, Eerdmans, 1951), p. 383.

[5] See, for example, Bk. II, chaps. 5, 12, 17, 21. The quotation is from chap. 12
in the S.D.F. Salmond translation in *The Nicene and Post-Nicene Fathers*, First
Series, ed. Philip Schaff, Vol. VI (New York, 1887; reprinted, Eerdmans, 1956),
p. 117. We quote from this translation throughout.

[6] See the collection of his comments in Reinhold Seeberg, *Textbook of the History of Doctrines* (2 vols. in 1; Philadelphia, 1905; reprinted, Baker Book House,
1952), II, 300–01. For a more recent treatment see Jaroslav Pelikan, *Luther the
Expositor* (St. Louis: Concordia, 1959), and Willem Jan Kooiman, *Luther and
the Bible* (Philadelphia: Muhlenberg, 1961).

[7] John Calvin, *Commentary on a Harmony of the Evangelists, Matthew, Mark,
and Luke,* trans. William Pringle (3 vols.; Edinburgh, 1845–46; reprinted,
Eerdmans, 1956), I, 258 f.

It is simply untrue, then, to affirm that the church throughout the centuries has maintained the inerrancy of the Bible in matters of fact. It should be added, however, that previous generations of Christians would have been puzzled by the extreme historical skepticism reflected in many modern commentaries on the Gospels.

III

If the biblical record does not present history inerrantly, can it be argued that its statement of kerygma is without error? This statement is much nearer the truth, but there are at least three difficulties which must still be met. *First,* taken by itself this formulation would be inadequate since it says nothing about history, and something must be said about history if biblical religion is to be taken seriously as historical religion. *Second,* the suggestion that the record is errant in connection with history but inerrant with respect to the kerygma results in an impossible bifurcation of Scripture. Is it possible to disentangle history from kerygma in this way? The crudest form of this hypothesis would mean that one verse or phrase is inerrant because it is kerygma, while the following verse is errant—or possibly errant—because it is only history. A more satisfactory division of the biblical materials would recognize that the same passage could be both history and kerygma, and that it could be inerrantly true as kerygma but only partially true, or possibly true, as history. Yet even this division of the text suggests impossibilities and absurdities. But the *third* difficulty is the most damaging. It arises when we ask whether even kerygmatic statements, or the kerygmatic aspect of statements, can rightly be referred to as "inerrant."

It may be more helpful if this question is put in the form of a concrete problem in New Testament interpretation. When we turn from the letters of Paul to the second chapter of James we discover a shift in theological perspective. In Paul we have been told that we are justified by faith and not by works (e.g., Gal.

3). But in James we are told, "So faith by itself, if it has no works, is dead" (James 2:17). Later it is stated even more emphatically: "For as the body apart from the spirit is dead, so faith apart from works is dead" (James 2:26). That is to say, "faith" corresponds to the body and "works" to the life-giving spirit in the body. So far as the last statement is concerned, it is fairly certain that Paul would have put the matter in precisely the opposite way. He would have said, "For as the body apart from the spirit is dead, so works apart from faith are dead." Faced with this apparent contradiction the student does some research. Some two dictionaries and three commentaries later he emerges with the conclusion that the terms "faith" and "works" do not mean the same thing in James and in Paul. Therefore so far as the *substance* of the matter is concerned, James 2 is not necessarily a direct contradiction of the Pauline concept, or vice versa. Yet it is far from certain that the author of James would have granted that his apparent difference with Paul was more semantic than theological, and it is probable that if Paul had read James his reaction would have been more violent than that of Luther!

Even so we are not yet out of the woods. By a particular interpretation of James it is possible to show that he was not directly contradicting Paul, since for him "faith" and "works" referred to concepts other than those which Paul associated with them. But when we return to James with the question, "How then *is* a man justified?" do we find any answer which, from the perspective of the Pauline tradition, could be called inerrant kerygma? Certainly the statement of James can be understood as one aspect of the truth, a chastening challenge to those carried away by an extreme or distorted Paulinism. It is meaningful as an element in the total kerygma which safeguards against a distortion of that totality. But is there any evidence that the author thought of it as an element in the kerygma rather than as the very essence of that kerygma? Whatever he may have intended, for me it is only a fragment of the total kerygma and therefore not, of itself, inerrant. Lest I be accused of establishing Paul as the bearer of the inerrant kerygma over against the other New Testament writers I hasten to add that his presentation also needs the correction or modification of emphasis provided by the other witnesses to the faith of the New Testament community. In a sense the message of each writer, or passage, is kerygma. But in a still deeper sense each of these statements of kerygma points toward the ultimate kerygma which is the reality beyond, and other than, any single or collective expression of it.

A second illustration of the "errancy" of kerygma is provided by a distinctive emphasis of the Book of Hebrews, namely, the doctrine of the impossibility of a second repentance. This doctrine is presented in Hebrews 6:4–8 and Hebrews 10:26–31. It is unlikely that any exegetical legerdemain can obscure the fact that these passages do indeed deny the possibility of a second repentance. On the second of these passages, Dr. Alexander C. Purdy is forced to conclude regretfully, "At this point . . . the author did not catch the full import of the gospel."[8] When we recreate the situation which existed in the second or third Christian generation we understand why the author of Hebrews sounds this solemn warning agaist apostasy, against turning away from the truth of God once it has been experienced. A phrase in the letter Pliny wrote to Trajan about the Christians indicates that before the end of the first century there were those who under pressure, or without pressure, had abandoned the new faith.[9] Pastors who have observed the dread hardening of hearts in individuals or groups know that there is a point beyond which repentance is impossible —except for the grace of God. But it is this grace on which we all depend! Can one really say that the literal formulation of the doctrine of the impossibility of a second repentance as it appears in Hebrews is inerrant kerygma? It is comforting to know that

[8] *The Interpreter's Bible* (12 vols.; New York and Nashville: Abingdon, 1952 ff.), XI, 715.
[9] See Henry Bettenson, *Documents of the Christian Church* (2nd ed.; Oxford University Press, 1963), p. 4.

this same question was raised by Martin Luther who, in his Preface to Hebrews, said that this teaching appeared "to be against all the Gospels and the Epistles of Paul. . . ." In the same Preface he praised the book as a whole because it contains "gold, silver, and precious stones"; he added, however, that it perhaps contains some "wood, straw or hay" along with these precious elements.[10]

Since the record does not present the history or the kerygma inerrantly, there is an inevitable tension between the record and the kerygma as well as between the record and the history. It is this tension which has provided the setting for the Quest for the historical Jesus and also the Quest for the Christ of faith.

Those who adopt the position which has been presented here are sometimes accused of attempting to judge Scripture by their own autonomous, human reason. Now any statement about Scripture, or about God, may reflect an arrogant, human pride. Most of us have on occasion been guilty of such pride. But when engaged in a debate with other Christians concerning the manner in which the Word of God confronts us in Scripture, it is difficult to understand why the judgments of those who challenge the inerrancy concept should be regarded as expressions of autonomous, human reason while the judgments of the defenders of that concept are exempted from that charge. Christians on both sides of this difference have heard and responded to the Word of God in Scripture. Both groups are attempting to formulate statements about Scripture which do justice to the fact that God's voice has been heard within these pages, but which do justice also to other facts known about these pages. The formulations of both sides reflect human judgments. It may *sound* more pious to say that the Word of God comes to us in Scripture without any human distortion, but this affirmation is a human judgment as fully as is its opposite. Human pride is best avoided by a humble willing-

---

[10] "Preface to the Epistle to the Hebrews," trans. C. M. Jacobs, *Works of Martin Luther,* Vol. VI (Philadelphia: Muhlenberg, 1932), p. 477.

ness to respond to whatever facts are known with a full awareness that still new facts may appear in the future.

IV

If a tension exists between the record, on the one hand, and
the history and the kerygma, on the other, what can be said of
the relation between history and kerygma? In the initial definition
of history and kerygma it was stated that they should be distinguished. But are they related so intimately that to know one
is to know the other? If the actual, external history were available
in all its richness, would the kerygma be self-evident to all men
of good will who might examine that history? To put the question in this way makes clear that only a negative answer is possible. Even if we could get at the history directly, the tension
between history and kerygma would still exist.

The kerygma was revealed to the community through the community's encounter with history, but the kerygma was not identical
with that history nor can it be deduced directly from that history
seen objectively as a series of events on the historical plane. This
is true both of the exodus and of the circle of events associated
with the ministry of Jesus. If Egyptian war correspondents had
reported on the progress of the exodus to the *Daily Papyrus* published back home in Rameses and Thebes, we can be quite certain
that these reports would not have contained very much kerygma
(at least not Israelite kerygma). Even if a neutral observer had
been present it is not clear that his reports would have contained
any kerygma. The kerygma was to be found on the "inside" of the
historical events, and not in their "outer" aspect, which could
have been recorded by a hostile or neutral observer. The events
were windows through which the Israelites glimpsed the mighty
acts of God, but a television camera would have captured only the
windows. Most of us to whom the biblical tradition speaks go
through a period of craving to discover "exactly what happened."
This craving stems not from any general historical curiosity, but

from an unconscious assumption that if we knew "exactly what happened" our religious faith would thereby be clarified and strengthened. Only later do we discover that "exactly what happened" was an outwardly ambiguous event, an event which, like others in history, is capable of two or more interpretations. It is when we have turned away from this initial question that we discover another question even more basic, namely, Does God lay hold of our lives as we heed the kerygma which was first heard by the believing community through its history?

What is true of the exodus story is equally true of the ministry of Jesus. "Behold, this child is set for the fall and rising of many in Israel, and for a sign that is spoken against . . ." (Luke 2:34). It is often stated that the resurrection appearances were only to believers. This is not a precise formulation of the evidence, since Paul was not a believer until after the appearance on the Damascus Road, and it is at least probable that the conversion of James, the brother of the Lord, occurred in connection with an appearance which he was granted.[11] More to the present issue is Matthew 28:17. Referring to a post-resurrection appearance of Jesus in Galilee, the text says, "And when they saw him they worshiped him; but some doubted." It is unimportant whether this is understood as a strictly accurate description of the response of former disciples to a single experience shortly after the crucifixion or whether it sums up the experience of the Christian community over a somewhat longer period of time. In either case it reflects the double response on the part of those most intimately associated with the events as they actually happened. It is clear that not all were convinced by the resurrection appearances, whatever form they may have taken. Faith and doubt contended for the mastery in the first eyewitnesses as well as in the later generations

---

[11] Cf. John 7:5; I Cor. 15:7; and Acts 1:14. However, Jerome in *On Illustrious Men*, chap. 2 (*The Nicene and Post-Nicene Fathers*, Second Series, ed. Philip Schaff and Henry Wace, Vol. III [New York, 1892; reprinted, Eerdmans, 1953], pp. 361 f.), reports a tradition taken from the Gospel of the Hebrews which implies that James was a believer in Jesus prior to this experience.

—and in ourselves. The kerygma was revealed in history, but the history did not compel or guarantee faith. This fact was often forgotten in the modern Quest for the historical Jesus, but it has come into the foreground in the twentieth century as a further complicating factor in the endeavor of the Christian community to clarify for itself and the world the relation between the record, the history, and the kerygma.

V

I have distinguished between record, history, and kerygma in the experience of revelation and in the tradition growing out of it, and have pointed to the tension between these three aspects of the total revelatory Event. I have suggested that the biblical record does not present inerrantly either the history or the kerygma, and, in a digression, have contended that though the kerygma is contained in the history it is not directly deducible from an objective account of that history.

Over the centuries when men and women have pondered the biblical record they have heard the kerygma, the Word of God, and their lives have been transformed by the judgment, forgiveness, and power of the God who met Israel in the exodus and who was and is the God and Father of our Lord Jesus Christ. While the doctrine of inerrancy in its traditional form cannot be maintained, the treasure it was created to protect is still there, hidden in the words of the record. In the Jewish tradition one of the famous sayings attributed to the "Men of the Great Synagogue" was, "Make a fence around the Torah." The enormous elaboration of oral regulations in the rabbinic system was intended to fence off the Torah with a protective, outer bulwark—a fence so strong and powerful that no one would break through to trespass against the commandments of the Torah itself. In light of the history of this attempt it is clear that this effort could not be permanently satisfactory. It may have served its purpose for a time, but it was a false way. In a real sense the doctrine of inerrancy has played a similar role in connection with Scripture, particularly in the Protestant tradition. The concept of inerrancy has been a symbol reminding Christians that there is a divine and not merely a human voice to be heard in the pages of Scripture. By their insistence that the very Word of God is to be heard in and through the words of Scripture the Fundamentalists have rendered us a service for which we should be grateful. It would only be fair to confess that they have maintained this view at times when, in some branches of Protestant theology, the Word of God was almost swallowed up by the words of men. But what was intended by some as a wall to protect the treasure has been for others a wall which has kept them away from that treasure.

The record does not present history or kerygma inerrantly, but it does present history and kerygma. It points toward that which happened and toward that which God was doing in what happened. It is witness to history and witness to kerygma. In the biblical record the writers did not distinguish between history and kerygma but wove the two together and witnessed to them using the methods or concepts of their own particular cultures. It has rightly been remarked that we do not look at the Scriptures but that we look with them to the God to whom they witness. We do not look at the words of Isaiah as ends in themselves, but we look with Isaiah—first, second, or third—to the God whom he saw. And standing with Isaiah we know that the Word of the Lord was not for him only but also for us and for all men. This is easy to state but not easy to put into practice. Children of the nineteenth century, with its historical-grammatical methods of interpretation, we look to the literal meaning of the words, afraid or unable to ask whether they point beyond themselves to the ways and work of God. Yet unless we look beyond the words, we discover that after all our labor the glory has departed.

Just as the language of a biblical writer is the language of his own age and place, so the categories of thought which he uses are those of his own milieu. If he writes history, he does not write it as it would have been written by a nineteenth-century scholar trained by Niebuhr or von Ranke at the University of Berlin. Such a methodology would have been meaningless to the biblical writer and to his initial readers, in fact to most of his readers throughout the past centuries. It may be that such a methodology will appear inadequate to readers of centuries lying beyond our own. The biblical writer wrote for his own day, with the skills and techniques of that day, though it should be added that his personal or communal experience with God transformed the methods and materials used. The opening chapters of Genesis reflect the ancient world from which they were borrowed, but they also reflect a transformation that occurred when these materials were put to the service of the faith of Israel. So the words of the record point us toward the culture from which they were drawn, but they also point beyond it to him who transcends all cultures even while he is present in them.

VI

Since the Jesus of history is not identical with the Jesus portrayed by the Gospels, Christian faith has from the beginning had hidden within its tradition a question concerning the historical Jesus. In periods when the church has been compelled to think carefully and critically about its foundations it has become aware of this hidden question and has sought to answer it with the skills and techniques available at the time. In the earliest centuries this hidden question was brought to the fore both by the intellectual challenge of the opposing pagan culture and by the diversities of opinion existing within the varied groups claiming the name Christian.

About A.D. 180 the pagan philosopher Celsus attacked the Christians in a major work called *The True Discourse*. This critique included theological and moral objections to Christianity but also an attack on the historical foundations of Judaism and Christianity. While *The True Discourse* has been lost, the bulk of it can be reproduced by combining the extensive quotations which appeared in the reply made, some sixty years later, by Origen in *Against Celsus*.[12] A century after Celsus the Neoplatonist philosopher Porphyry renewed the attack on Christianity in his treatise *Against the Christians,* referring, among other things, to the apparent contradictions within the Gospels. The church responded with a whole series of replies by men such as Methodius of Olympus, Eusebius of Caesarea, Apollinaris of Laodicea, Macarius Magnes, and Philostorgius. By a curious literary fate nearly all of these documents have vanished except for isolated fragments.[13]

Perhaps even more perplexing for the church were the diverse presentations of Jesus which appeared among Christian groups. It was in part in response to this confusion that the church determined to limit to four the Gospels to be accepted as canonical and authoritative, a development which will be traced in the following chapter.

With the political triumph of the church in the fourth century, and its consolidation against fringe groups, the intellectual challenges to its faith lessened, although inner theological struggles continued. The following centuries offer little evidence of any awareness that the discovery of the historical Jesus involved a Quest. He is assumed to be known or easily knowable. Where an interest in the Jesus of history appears it is an interest in finding didactic or devotional methods for presenting him to a believing but ill-informed public.[14] Interest in the human life of Jesus was kept alive, however, by groups such as the Cistercians and the Franciscans.

[12] See the modern translation by Henry Chadwick (Cambridge University Press, 1953).
[13] The most useful known evidence for the views of Porphyry and those of his opponents is *The Apocritus of Macarius Magnes,* trans. and ed. T. W. Crafer (London: S.P.C.K., 1919). For brief notes (including biographical references) on other replies to Porphyry, see Johannes Quasten, *Patrology* (Westminster, Md.: Newman, 1960), III, 333, 377, 486–88, 530–32.
[14] See chapter 3 below.

With the Renaissance came a whole new curiosity about all things human, including the humanity of Jesus. Undoubtedly this played a major role in the blossoming of Gospel harmonies in the sixteenth century.[15] It was not until the late eighteenth century, however, that the Quest for the historical Jesus became a veritable passion absorbing a large proportion of the intellectual energies of the church. This movement in the life of the church paralleled and reflected the emergence of historiography as an independent, specialized, self-conscious, and highly developed discipline. It is difficult for us of the twentieth century to remember how recently modern historiography was born. *A Guide to Historical Method* by Gilbert J. Garraghan, S.J., offers some illuminating insights in this respect.[16] By a careful reading of Garraghan's observations in the section "Bibliography of Historical Method"[17] it is possible to date the appearance of the various elements essential to this modern discipline. One notes, in the sixteenth century, a recognition of the all-important distinction between primary and secondary sources. The seventeenth century produced the claim that "history" had a right to a separate place alongside of the other academic disciplines; this century also saw the first systematic consideration of textual criticism. In the mid-eighteenth century historians were warned that even an honest eyewitness may report inaccurately because of errors in perception. But it was in the nineteenth century that the new discipline came into its full glory.[18] It was against this background that the modern Quest for the historical Jesus developed, and it is against this background that the Quest must be understood.

---

[15] See chapter 4 below.

[16] Edited by Jean Delanglez, S. J. (New York: Fordham University Press, 1946).

[17] *Ibid.*, pp. 427–31. See also pp. 59–69.

[18] It must not be imagined that no valid historical work was done before this time, or that the techniques of nineteenth-century historiography represent the ultimate in the understanding of history.

2

The Earliest Phase
of the
Quest

During the first four centuries of the Christian era there were at least two movements which may be described as phases of the Quest for the historical Jesus. The first of these led to the establishment of the four Gospels as the canonical authorities for the reconstruction of the life and ministry of Jesus. An initial step in all historical research is the discovery of the available sources and their classification into primary and secondary groups. While this was not the language the church used to describe its canonization of Matthew, Mark, Luke, and John, the effect of this canonization was to establish these books as the primary sources for the life of Jesus. Modern research has made it difficult to believe that even the first and the fourth Gospels, which tradition had always ascribed to Matthew and John, were written by actual eyewitnesses of the ministry. Nevertheless these four contain old tradition, some of which no doubt goes back to eyewitnesses. In this sense, and in the sense that the four are the best witnesses available, one may speak of them as primary sources. The second movement during these first four centuries was the attempt to weave the diverse traditions contained in the four Gospels into a single, unified "Life of Jesus." The efforts made in this direction are interesting and may have been the necessary, first experiments. Comparatively speaking, however, these experiments were failures, since the church did not understand the true relationship of the Gospels to each other or the nature of the traditions which they contained.

I

The average Christian is only dimly aware that there were numerous other books which might have been used alongside of, or even instead of, the four Gospels which are now in the New Testament. The discovery of Coptic, Gnostic gospels at Cheno-boskion, and the newspaper publicity given especially to the Gos-pel of Thomas, have been sufficient to remind many Christians that they had indeed heard of "apocryphal gospels," or, perhaps, of "the lost books of the Bible." Yet it is generally assumed that our four Gospels were universally accepted as the earliest Gospels and that the other would-be gospels were later products, pale or bizarre imitations of the originals. Certainly many of the apocryphal gospels did originate well after our four, found acceptance only in limited circles, and were pale or bizarre or both if judged by historical, theological, or literary standards. Thus there is considerable truth in this comfortable assumption, but it is not the whole truth with respect to the apocryphal gospels.

The best modern survey of these gospels is the first volume of Edgar Hennecke's *New Testament Apocrypha*.[1] Some fifty apocryphal gospels are presented in this volume, at least in excerpt form. Many of these were comparatively late products of Christian speculation or imagination and never achieved real significance in the life of the church. But some were genuine rivals of our four, offering them serious competition for a place

[1] Third German edition edited by Wilhelm Schneemelcher; English translation edited by R. McL. Wilson (Philadelphia: Westminster, 1963).

in the canon.[2] We want to ask four questions concerning the canonical and apocryphal gospels:

1. When were our four Gospels generally accepted as authoritative?
2. What gospels were in circulation prior to that time?
3. What was the status of the various gospels before those presently in the New Testament received general acceptance?
4. Why were the canonical four accorded that position?

The first of these questions is the simplest to answer. It is clear that by the end of the second century Matthew, Mark, Luke, and John were widely regarded as authoritative throughout the major geographical divisions of the church. To what extent this may have been true even earlier will be considered under question three. About A.D. 175, Irenaeus, Bishop of Lyons, in a passage more rhetorical than logical insisted there must be four and precisely four Gospels just as there are four directions here on earth, north, south, east, and west. He also linked the four Gospels with the four beasts mentioned in Revelation 4:7,[3] though he may not have been the first to make this identification which has proved so tenacious in the tradition of the church. Near the turn of the century Tertullian of North Africa, Clement of Alexandria, and Origen, also of Alexandria, all recognized our four Gospels as those normative for the church's understanding of Jesus. In addition to the witness of this "Big Four" about A.D. 200, there is the testimony of the Muratorian Canon which reflects, presumably, the Roman situation about A.D. 175.[4] The

[2] Useful books on the formation and composition of the canon include Alexander Souter, *The Text and Canon of the New Testament* (rev. ed. by C. S. C. Williams; London: Gerald Duckworth, 1954) ; and Floyd V. Filson, *Which Books Belong in the Bible?* (Philadelphia: Westminster, 1957).

[3] Irenaeus, *Against Here. ies,* Bk. III, chap. 11, sec. 8; trans. and ed. A. Roberts and J. Donaldson in *The Ante-Nicene Fathers,* Vol. I (New York, 1899; reprinted, Eerdmans, 1953), p. 428.

[4] In 1740 L. A. Muratori published an eighth-century manuscript he had discovered which contained this partial list of New Testament books. The list is believed to have been prepared in Rome toward the end of the second century. If so, it is the earliest "list" of New Testament books.

canon is only a fragment and it does not mention Matthew or
Mark explicitly, but it does identify Luke and John as the third
and fourth Gospels. Furthermore, the fragment which precedes
the comments on Luke seems to refer to Mark. The importance
of these five witnesses—and perhaps a sixth, the Anti-Marcionite
Prologues—is that they represent different geographical areas of
the church, i.e., Alexandria, North Africa, Rome, Asia Minor, and
Gaul. While in some local areas the four may not have been
used, and elsewhere additional gospels may have been popular, it
is clear that our canonical four were accepted as normative Gospels
in the major centers of the church by or before A.D. 200.

The second question is: What gospels were in circulation prior
to the general acceptance of the four, or, as we may now say, prior
to A.D. 200? Luke's Prologue contains the earliest explicit evidence
that gospels—or gospel-like documents other than those in our
canon—existed while the evangelists were doing their work.
"Inasmuch as many have undertaken to compile a narrative of
the things which have been accomplished among us, just as they
were delivered to us by those who from the beginning were eyewitnesses and ministers of the word, it seemed good to me also
. . ." (Luke 1:1–3a). Parallels to Luke's opening phrase in other
Hellenistic historians suggest that he was following a literary
convention in some of the phraseology he employed and that
his "many" may mean only "several." But even this would
imply that he was acquainted with at least three or four accounts
of Jesus' ministry, or parts of that ministry. It is generally assumed that one of these accounts was our Gospel of Mark. Even
if Luke knew Matthew, which is unlikely, he must then have
referred to still other documents. That is to say, he must have
known gospels other than those presently in our canon.

This implication of the Prologue was quickly recognized by
scholars within the church. Early in the third century, Origen, in
the first of his *Homilies on Luke,* spoke scornfully of the "many"

who had "undertaken" or "attempted" to write gospels.[5] According to Origen's interpretation these "many" had been unsuccessful in what they "attempted" because they had not been guided by the Holy Spirit. The four evangelists, on the other hand, had been successful because their work had been carried out with the active assistance of the Holy Spirit. In the same context[6] Origen mentions five examples of such unsuccessful gospels: The Gospel According to the Egyptians, The Gospel According to the Twelve Apostles, The Gospel According to Thomas, The Gospel According to Basilides, and The Gospel According to Matthias. He indicated that there were still other such gospels.

The critics of Christianity also noted this multiplicity of gospels. Celsus, writing before A.D. 200, jeered at the Christians for having "corrupted their Gospel from its original integrity to a three-fold, and four-fold, and many-fold degree. . . ."[7] Origen's comments suggest that he understood Celsus to refer to changes made in the texts of the Gospels, but it is likely that Celsus also had reference to the number and variety of gospels appearing. It must be remembered that originally the term "Gospel" was used by the Christians exclusively in the singular, to refer to the message of and about Jesus. When books appeared with accounts of Jesus' ministry, the singular was at first preserved in titles such as "The Gospel According to Matthew" or "The Gospel According to Luke," implying that there was only one Gospel but more than one witness to it. By the middle of the second century, however, individual books themselves were being called "Gospels," the term being used in the plural.[8] Outsiders, noting the differ-

[5] A critical edition of the Greek and Latin texts of the *Homilies* is available in Max Rauer (ed.), *Origenes Werke*, Vol. IX ("Die griechischen christlichen Schriftsteller der ersten Jahrhunderten," No. 49; Berlin: Akademie-Verlag, 1959) ; the text of the first Homily is given on pp. 3–11.

[6] *Ibid.,* pp. 4 f.

[7] Quoted in Origen, *Against Celsus,* Bk. II, chap. 27; we cite from the translation in *The Ante-Nicene Fathers,* Vol. IV (New York, 1902; reprinted, Eerdmans, 1951), p. 443.

[8] This is the usage in chaps. 66 and 67 of the *First Apology* of Justin Martyr (*ca.* A.D. 100–*ca.* 165).

ences in fact and theology between the various books, charged that the one Gospel, i.e., the one message, had become many Gospels, i.e., many different messages. Marcion, in the middle of the second century, used only one Gospel—a version of Luke —and quoted Scripture (Rom. 2:16) to support his contention that there should be only one written Gospel.[9]

From various sources it is known that still other gospels were in circulation before A.D. 200, e.g., The Gospel of the Hebrews, The Gospel of the Nazarenes, The Gospel of Peter, The Ebionite Gospel, The Gospel of Truth (sometimes attributed to Valentinus), Protevangelium of James, and possibly a considerable number of others, particularly some now known from the Coptic, Gnostic Library at Chenoboskion.

Thus by A.D. 200, when the canonical four were unquestionably accepted in the major centers of the church, there must have been at least a dozen other gospels in circulation. Perhaps a majority of them had been written after the last of the four, but this cannot be true of those referred to in Luke's Prologue, nor is it necessarily true of some of the others, e.g., the so-called Jewish or Ebionite gospels.

Our third question is: What was the status of the various gospels prior to the emergence of the canonical four as authoritative at the end of the second century? Broadly speaking two contrasting answers are given to this question. For convenience, but without prejudice, we may label these the conservative and the radical answers. The radical answer is ably represented by Oscar Cullmann's article "The Plurality of the Gospels as a Theological Problem in Antiquity" which appeared in translation in his book of essays *The Early Church*.[10] The conservative answer was set forth by way of reply to Cullmann by a Roman Catholic scholar,

[9] Cf. Origen, *Commentary on John*, Bk. V, sec. 4 (*The Ante-Nicene Fathers*, Vol. IX [New York, 1896], p. 348).

[10] Trans. A. J. B. Higgins and Stanley Godman (Philadelphia: Westminster, 1956).

J. H. Crehan, S.J., in a paper presented at the 1957 Oxford International Congress on the Four Gospels.[11] In brief the conservative answer holds that the four Gospels now in the New Testament were generally accepted as authoritative in the major centers of the church throughout the second century and not simply in the latter part of that century. The radical answer insists that for much of the second century it is likely that a wide diversity of attitudes existed: some centers may have accepted all four Gospels, others may have recognized only one, while still others may have used gospels later excluded from the canon. I can only summarize the arguments involved in the discussion, and in this summary I have not always followed the presentation of Cullmann or Crehan. And that six arguments are presented on each side is not necessarily a guarantee of objectivity!

In support of the conservative answer are the following considerations:

1. There is a tradition that John reviewed the first three Gospels in Ephesus, gave them their titles, and then prepared a fourth Gospel to fill their gaps and to interpret more accurately the history recorded. While the full form of this tradition is from the fourth century (*Acta Timothei*), Father Crehan points out that it may be traced back through Eusebius to Origen and possibly even to the Muratorian Canon. Even if the tradition is not itself historical, its existence reflects a period when the four Gospels were generally accepted as authoritative.

2. Tatian's *Diatessaron*, prepared about A.D. 170, used the four Gospels, thus indicating their primacy at that time.

3. Irenaeus, about A.D. 175, identified the four Gospels with the four beasts of Revelation 4:7. Father Crehan feels this identification may be traced back to Papias (*ca.* A.D. 60–130). (It was also used by Victorinus of Pettau, *ca.* A.D. 300, who, presumably, did not know Irenaeus but did know Papias.) If Papias used the

---

[11] Published as "The Fourfold Character of the Gospel" in *The Gospels Reconsidered* (Oxford: Blackwell, 1960), pp. 36–46.

beasts of Revelation 4:7 as symbols of the Gospels it proves that the four occupied a unique position before the middle of the second century.

4. The unanimous testimony of Irenaeus, the Muratorian Canon, and the Anti-Marcionite Prologues, all before A.D. 200, must mean that the four Gospels were solidly established in the life of the church well before that date.

5. Justin Martyr, in the middle of the second century, speaks of gospels written by "apostles" and by "those who followed them."[12] The plural form in each case suggests that he included more than one gospel in each category, and this fits the theory that two Gospels were written by "apostles" (Matthew and John) and two by "those who followed them" (Mark and Luke).

6. It is generally agreed that Mark 16:9–20 was not an original part of that Gospel but was added to it, possibly before the end of the second century.[13] It is probable that these additional verses were created as a composite narrative taken from the endings of Matthew, Luke, and John. That this was done before the end of the second century would indicate the unique position occupied by these Gospels at that time.

Those who support a more radical view of the status of the four Gospels during the second century would reply to the above arguments by saying that they provide evidence for a fairly widespread use of these four in the closing decades of the second century but that they certainly do not allow one to draw conclusions about the situation during the first half of that century. Thus, the supporters of this view would say it is sheer speculation to assert that Papias applied Revelation 4:7 to the Gospels; moreover, the Anti-Marcionite Prologues may not be from the second century, while Mark 16:9–20 may be later than the period assumed for it and, furthermore, may have included material from outside the four Gospels. As for the evidence of Justin, it

---

[12] *Dialogue with Trypho,* chap. 103 (*The Ante-Nicene Fathers,* Vol. I).
[13] Cf. the Latin text of Irenaeus, *op. cit.,* Bk. III, chap. 10, sec. 6.

is too limited to permit any conclusion concerning the *number* of gospels he regarded as authoritative.

In support of the more radical position the following considerations may be advanced:

1. The Gospel of Matthew, and possibly that of Luke, was intended to replace Mark rather than to coexist with it.

2. In Eusebius' *Ecclesiastical History*[14] the famous Papias passage apparently contrasts the written word with the oral tradition to the disparagement of the former; this disparagement is scarcely compatible with any theory that Papias regarded the four Gospels as authoritative. Furthermore, since Eusebius quotes him only in connection with Matthew and Mark, it may be that Papias did not know or recognize Luke or John. Finally, Papias did use the Gospel of the Hebrews. Conclusion: Papias did not recognize our fourfold Gospel canon.

3. Justin Martyr does not seem to have used the Gospel of John.

4. Irenaeus[15] states that the Ebionites used only Matthew, while other groups used only Mark, and some of the Valentinians used only John.

5. There is at least some evidence that Palestinian Christians used only Matthew, while Gentile Christians in Egypt used chiefly the Gospel of the Egyptians.[16]

6. The rhetorical character of Irenaeus' argument for a fourfold Gospel canon suggests (a) that this fourfold canon was *not* universally recognized when he wrote, and (b) that he was not able to appeal to a truly long-standing tradition in support of his position.

It is difficult to achieve a balanced judgment between these various possibilities. The use of one Gospel, as over against the four, appears to have been a characteristic chiefly of fringe

---

[14] Bk. III, chap. 39, sec. 4.
[15] *Op. cit.,* Book III, chap. 11, sec. 7.
[16] See Cullman, *The Early Church,* p. 45.

groups within the church or on the borders of the church. But is it possible, in the early second century, to distinguish sharply between "the church" and "fringe groups"? On the other hand, the acceptance of all four Gospels cannot be demonstrated definitely for any segment of the church before the second half of the second century. It is likely that this fourfold canon was emerging in the middle of that century, though whether before or only after Marcion's canon cannot be determined. It remains a tantalizing question whether Marcion with his one Gospel and ten Pauline letters presented a reduced canon which was then restored to its original fullness, or whether Marcion had the first New Testament canon, one which the church subsequently "trumped" by producing a more inclusive list, i.e., not just one Gospel but four, not just ten Pauline letters but thirteen (fourteen), not letters of just one apostle (Paul) but letters also from James, Peter, Jude, and John.

Our final question about the emergence of the four Gospels as canonical is: Why were precisely these four accepted as authoritative?

Perhaps the only theologically satisfying answer is that the church made its decision through the guidance of the Holy Spirit. But since the Holy Spirit did not cast a direct "vote" in such matters, the question remains through what channels or types of reasoning the Holy Spirit guided the churches. In a passage already alluded to,[17] Origen insisted that these four Gospels were distinguished from their rivals by the fact that they were written by the power of the Holy Spirit and were not products of merely human wisdom. But what characteristics of the Gospels led him to this conclusion? If some of the church Fathers had been asked why Matthew, Mark, Luke, and John were included in the canon while other Gospels were excluded, they would doubtless have replied that the canonical four were written by apostolic men,

[17] See above p. 28–29.

i.e., by apostles or men closely associated with them. Irenaeus, writing about A.D. 175, clearly differentiates the four Gospels from other such documents on the grounds that these four have "apostolic" sanction. Thus in the opening sections of Book II of *Against Heresies* he states:

> For the Lord of all gave to His apostles the power of the Gospel, through whom also we have known the truth, that is, the doctrine of the Son of God; to whom also did the Lord declare: "He that heareth you heareth Me; and he that despiseth you, despiseth Me, and Him that sent Me."
>
> We have learned from none others the plan of our salvation, than from those through whom the Gospel has come down to us, which they did at one time proclaim in public, and, at a later period, by the Will of God, handed down to us in the Scriptures, to be the ground and pillar of our faith.[18]

Then, a few lines later, Irenaeus comments on the authorship of the four Gospels. The implication of the passage is that these Gospels, and these alone, are authoritative because they alone were the product of the apostolic tradition.

Thus Irenaeus suggests that the four Gospels were authoritative because they were apostolic, and that they were apostolic because they were written by "apostolic" men. But did the church in general regard the Gospels as "apostolic" (a) because they had concrete, historical evidence of their authorship; or (b) because these Gospels were used in "apostolic" churches; or (c) because these four, unlike the others, conformed with apostolic tradition as it was currently understood? Perhaps all these factors were involved in differing measures, or perhaps it was their assumed convergence that established the authority of the four Gospels.

Eusebius[19] tells an intriguing story of Serapion, Bishop of Antioch at the end of the second century. Learning that the

---

[18] Translation from *The Ante-Nicene Fathers*, I, 359.
[19] Eusebius, *Ecclesiastical History,* Bk. VI, chap. 12.

Gospel of Peter was in common use among the Christians of Rhossus in Cilicia, he gave permission for this use to continue. Later, having become convinced that the Gospel of Peter was strongly "docetic," he ordered its use discontinued. In writing about the incident, Serapion clearly assumes that the gospel was falsely attributed to Peter; but it is not clear whether this had been his assumption all along or whether it emerged only when he determined the character of the document. It is likely that the question of authorship was wholly secondary to that of orthodoxy; that is to say, for Serapion the unorthodox character of the document determined its non-Petrine authorship.

Another factor in the canonization of the four Gospels was their use in the worship services of the church. It can be argued that the liturgy was the hallway to the canon. In the middle of the second century Justin Martyr stated that the "memoirs of the apostles" were also known as "Gospels."[20] In a succeeding passage he says:

> And on the day called Sunday, all who live in cities or in the country gather together to one place, and the memoirs of the apostles or the writings of the prophets are read, as long as time permits.[21]

Presumably this refers to the reading of passages from the Gospels and from the Old Testament. From the beginning the words of the Lord had possessed an authority at least equal to that of the Old Testament. Now as the Gospels, i.e., books enshrining the "words of the Lord," were read in the services of worship along with the Old Testament, the books themselves came to be recognized as equally authoritative. Liturgical use established canonical authority.

In this connection it is significant that the Muratorian Canon, referring to a book still disputed in the church, says that it is one "which some of our people do not want to have read in the

---

[20] *First Apology*, chap. 66.
[21] *Ibid.*, chap. 67 (translation from *The Ante-Nicene Fathers*, I, 186).

Church."[22] This is another illustration of the link between liturgy and canonicity.

The details will never be certain unless new second-century sources are discovered, but we will not be far wrong if we say that our four Gospels came to be recognized as authoritative (a) because they were widely used in the services of worship; (b) because they were regarded as the work of apostolic men; and (c) because they conformed to the "rule of faith" which was emerging in response to the controversies of the second century (i.e., the Gospels steered a middle way between Gnosticism and Ebionism).[23] Since these developments occurred prior to the period of the great church councils they were the expression of a growing consensus rather than of a conciliar decision. Probably the choice was governed more by the theological controversies of the day than by any awareness of historical methodology, but the choice was, nevertheless, basically valid because the decisive centers of church life were still in close touch with the historical tradition originating in Jesus of Nazareth.

Whatever factors, human or divine, led to the selection of these four out of the many gospels in circulation, the church must be forever grateful that this particular choice was made. In the many apocryphal gospels now known, half of which have been recovered only in our own generation, there may be stray incidents or sayings which shed light on him whom we call the Christ. But the overwhelming proportion of this material in the apocryphal gospels reflects only the subsequent developments in the life of the church. It is still true that the Quest for the historical Jesus must begin, and to a large extent end, with the study of the four canonical Gospels. Had one or more of these four been omitted the Quest would have been made that much more difficult. From the perspective of the Quest the only significant

[22] Translation from Hennecke-Schneemelcher, *New Testament Apocrypha,* I, 45.
[23] Gnosticism, with its speculative, theological interests, dealt somewhat cavalierly with history; Ebionism, a form of Jesus Christianity, had a lower Christology than that which prevailed in the main tradition of the church.

criticism of the early church is that it did not sufficiently encourage the preservation of still other books which, though secondary, might still have been of assistance to historians.

II

The first task in any project of historical research is to gather
the primary sources. By the end of the second century this had
been completed. Already before it had been completed a second task
had begun to emerge. If the four Gospels were authoritative, how
were the various narratives to be combined into a unified whole?
The same problem confronts any modern writer who attempts
a "Life" of Jesus. However, the modern writer, if he is at all con-
versant with source criticism and form criticism, knows that the
task of synthesizing can be carried out only after literary and
historical criticism have completed their work on the individual
Gospels. The scholars of the first centuries after Christ attempted
to use all four Gospels as they stand, modifying them only when
tension between one Gospel and another was so obvious as to
demand attention. While the scholars of this period made innumerable shrewd and helpful observations, and were ingenious
in their attempted solutions of problems, their assumptions that
the four Gospels represented four independent witnesses and
that these witnesses presented basically firsthand tradition vitiated
their methods for harmonizing the materials.

The following pages will discuss three early attempts to create
a unified "Life" of Christ out of the materials provided by the
fourfold Gospel tradition: first, the *Diatessaron* of Tatian, from
about A.D. 170; second, the Eusebian Sections and Canons from
A.D. 325; and, third, Augustine's influential study, *On the Harmony of the Gospels,* written about A.D. 400. It should be added
that during this same period there were still other attempts to
deal with this problem. Thus some believe that Justin Martyr,
the teacher of Tatian, used a harmony of the Gospels. If so, it
cannot now be reconstructed, though it may have influenced

Tatian's work. According to Jerome,[24] Theophilus of Antioch (*ca.* A.D. 180) also composed a harmony, while Eusebius of Caesarea affirms that Ammonius of Alexandria (third century) prepared a commentary on Matthew which indicated, in some way, the parallel passages from the other Gospels.[25] However, the first three works we have cited had the greatest continuing influence, and it is these that will be considered here.

If Tatian's *Diatessaron* was not the first Gospel harmony it certainly was the most successful.[26] But first a word about Tatian himself. Born a Syrian, educated in various religious and philosophic traditions, he was converted to Christianity, possibly in Rome, and worked with Justin. About A.D. 172 he returned to Syria and was associated with the Encratites, a group with ascetic and Gnostic tendencies. At some time in his career he prepared a harmony of the Gospels. This *Diatessaron* was widely used in the Syrian church, instead of the four separate Gospels, until as late as the fifth century when it was displaced by the Syriac Peshitta. Theodoret, who became Bishop of Cyrrhus about A.D. 423, reported that he destroyed some 200 copies of the *Diatessaron* in the communities under his care. Such zeal may have been beneficial for his churches, but it complicated the task of the modern scholar, who is as yet without a Syriac copy of the *Diatessaron*. The objections to the *Diatessaron* were (a) a preference for the traditional fourfold version of the Gospel narrative, and (b) the charge of Encratite heresy which stood against its author, a heresy which was thought to have influenced the text of the *Diatessaron* at some points (e.g., in the omission of the genealogies).

Nevertheless, as previously stated, the *Diatessaron* became the most successful harmony in Christian history. Over the centuries

[24] Letter 121:6, 15 (J. P. Migne, *Patrologia Latina* [221 vols.; Paris, 1844 ff.], XXI, 1018 ff.).

[25] See Eusebius, *Letter to Carpianus*. (The letter is reproduced in Greek in the Introduction to the Nestle-Aland Greek New Testament.)

[26] The term *Diatessaron* is from the Greek and means, literally, "through the four."

it was translated into many languages. It undoubtedly existed in Syriac, Greek, Latin, Armenian, Arabic, Persian, Coptic, Dutch, Italian, Middle English, and various forms of German. It probably existed in French, and there may well have been other versions of which no trace exists today. Some who translated it, and many who used it, were unaware of its associations with Tatian—if they even knew who Tatian was. The *Diatessaron* circulated in these various versions for well over a thousand years. In fact, until the sixteenth century only a few other Gospel harmonies achieved any recognition whatsoever.[27] Its influence may be traced beyond the boundaries of Gospel harmonies in the strict sense, for example, in the ninth century *Heliand* or in Otfrid von Weissenberg's *Liber Evangeliorum.*

Despite this widespread usage the disappearance of the Syriac text of the *Diatessaron* has created a series of unanswered questions, so that the study of the *Diatessaron* has been described as "a shoreless ocean of research." Having spent some months paddling a canoe on that ocean I am convinced this description is not inaccurate. Some of the still unanswered questions are these:

1. In what language was the *Diatessaron* composed, Greek or Syriac?

2. What was the original order of the narrative?

3. Did Tatian use only the four Gospels, or was there a fifth Gospel which may even have given him his outline?

4. What was the original text of any given passage? (This is the question which has most concerned the scholars.)

5. Was Tatian's work original, or was it based on still earlier efforts toward a harmony, perhaps a harmony used by Justin?

6. Did Tatian conceive of his work as a substitute for the four Gospels or as a guide to their interpretation?

Fortunately, only two of these questions are indispensable for

[27] There were exceptions, such as the Harmony of Guido von Perpignan (*ca.* 1320) and that of John Gerson (*ca.* 1400).

our purpose: How many Gospels did Tatian use, and what was
the original order of the narrative? With respect to the first question I shall side with the majority of scholars and assert dog-
matically that the *Diatessaron* was based solely on the four canonical Gospels. The name *Diatessaron* is not of itself conclusive
since it may not have been Tatian's own title, but its use reflects
the impression made by the document on early readers. The traces
of elements not in our canonical Gospels do not seem to justify
the hypothesis of a fifth Gospel source, despite the ardent con-
tentions of Curt Peters.[28]

The question of order cannot be handled so apodictically.
When the *Diatessaron* was translated, and possibly when it was
copied, those carrying out this task felt free to revise the order
found in the manuscript, presumably in favor of a tradition with
which they were familiar in their own communities. The result
is that the various versions differ significantly in the sequence
of incidents. The Arabic version and Ephraem's Commentary on
the *Diatessaron* are generally regarded as the best guides to Tatian's original order, though, unfortunately, Ephraem's Commentary has been extant only in an Armenian translation. Recently a Syriac manuscript was discovered containing substantial
portions of the Commentary.[29] In general its order confirms that
previously known through the Armenian translation. A study by
Louis Leloir[30] provides the most useful survey on the question
of order. This study presents in tabular form the sequence in
Ephraem's Commentary, while parallel columns indicate the location of the same materials in the Arabic, Latin, Dutch, Italian
(Venetian), and Persian versions. The following comments are
based on the order of the Arabic version plus Ephraem's Com-

[28] *Das Diatessaron Tatians* ("Orientalia Christiana Analecta," No. 123; Rome:
Pontificum Institutum Orientalium Studiorum, 1939).

[29] S. Éphrem, *Commentaire de l'Évangile concordant. Texte syriaque. Manu-
scrit Chester Beatty 709* (Dublin, 1962).

[30] *Le Témoignage d' Éphrem sur le Diatessaron* ("Corups Scriptorum Christian-
orum Orientalium," No. 227; Louvain, 1962), pp. 1–11.

mentary, or, if Ephraem is lacking, the Arabic alone.[31]

Whatever the details of the original order may have been it is clear that Tatian dealt comparatively freely with the Gospel sequences. He adapted the order of one Gospel to fit that of another Gospel or of a pattern which he regarded as superior to that of any one Gospel. It is sometimes stated that Tatian adopted the three Passovers of John's Gospel, but this is to oversimplify. In John's Gospel the first recorded Passover is associated with the cleansing of the temple (John 2). But Tatian combined the Johannine and the Synoptic cleansings, placing them near the end of Jesus' ministry; therefore he has no reference corresponding to John 2:13–16. (Incidentally, Tatian also placed the Nicodemus story in the latter part of Jesus' ministry.) In other words *if* Tatian had three Passovers they are not the same as the Johannine three. I say "if" because only two are explicitly mentioned in the text. Tatian's first Passover was in connection with the feeding of the five thousand (18:24), and the final Passover was, of course, in connection with Jesus' concluding ministry in Jerusalem (39:1 ff.). However, the logic of Tatian's pattern implies another Passover between these two, for 30:31 refers to the Feast of Unleavened Bread and this Feast cannot be immediately after the Passover of 18:24 since, in addition to the many incidents intervening, a Feast of Tabernacles is mentioned in 29:1, 9. The problem of the length of Jesus' ministry may not have concerned Tatian at all, and he might have been puzzled had he been asked whether he followed the Synoptic or the Johannine chronology. Attempting to incorporate all the material in the four Gospels, he inevitably included more Feasts than the Synoptists, but he may have been unconcerned with the number of Passovers or years implied. He did not equate the Johannine cleansing with that in the Synoptics in order to eliminate a Johannine Passover but, rather, because he regarded the two cleansings

<hr>

[31] The references in the text are to the translation of the Arabic by H. W. Hogg in *The Ante-Nicene Fathers*, Vol. IX (New York, 1896), pp. 35–138.

as so similar that they should be identified.

In general Tatian tended to combine narratives in one Gospel with similar narratives elsewhere, even if they did not appear in the same chronological sequence in the two Gospels or even if they differed in some details. Thus he combined the healing of the centurion's servant in Matthew 8 and Luke 7 with the similar story in John 4. Most of the Lucan parallels to the Sermon on the Mount are conflated with Matthew 5–7. The question of the greatest commandment in Luke 10:25–37 (including the parable of the Good Samaritan) is transferred to the latter part of Jesus' ministry and combined with Mark 12:28–31 and parallels. The parable of the great supper in Luke 14 is identified with Matthew's parable of the marriage feast and placed near the end of the ministry. The three Synoptic accounts of the healing of the blind man (men) near Jericho are treated as a single incident. On the other hand the parable of the pounds in Luke 19 is differentiated from that of the talents in Matthew 25, and the anointing of Jesus in Luke 7 is treated as a separate incident from the anointing near the close of the ministry; in the latter incident Matthew, Mark, and John are combined despite chronological difficulty.

When the experts are asked which Gospel provided the basic outline for Tatian, two different answers are given; some say Matthew, others say John. This uncertainty may reflect the fact that Tatian did not consciously select any one of the Gospels for his chronological guide. Any harmonist attempting to give equal weight to all four Gospels would come out about where Tatian did, since Matthew and John have the "strong" chronologies, while Mark is similar to Matthew, and Luke's central section (Luke 9:51—18:14) is chronologically formless.

The Tatian enthusiasts insist that he did a magnificent job of combining the details of parallel pericopes into unified and polished mosaics. This may well be correct, though a fairer evaluation of this judgment will be possible only when substantial portions of the original text have been recovered.

By way of summary it may be said that Tatian attempted to create a unified "Life" of Jesus by including practically everything from the four Gospels; he combined incidents if they were at all similar without too much concern for differences in chronology or detail; and, consciously or unconsciously, he allowed the chronologies of Matthew and John to dominate his pattern.

III

Every theological student who uses Nestle's text of the Greek New Testament has his attention called to the numbers on the inner margins of that text. Actually there are two sets of numbers located there, but the ones which concern us are those from the Canons and Sections of Eusebius. These are described in Eusebius' *Letter to Carpianus* written about A.D. 325. In his letter Eusebius stated that a certain Ammonius had prepared a fourfold Gospel by placing alongside a copy of Matthew the parallel passages from the other three Gospels. Eusebius pointed out that this arrangement disturbed the sequence of the Gospels other than Matthew. He did not mention that if Ammonius included *only* the material parallel to Matthew he must have omitted entirely a few sections from Mark, many more from Luke, and the bulk of John. This omission from the criticism of Eusebius is puzzling, and it is conceivable that Ammonius actually created a form of harmony using all the material in the four Gospels but arranging it according to the order of Matthew. However, the work of Ammonius has vanished, and we are concerned with that of Eusebius. After pointing out the weakness of Ammonius' method Eusebius stated that, spurred on by this example, he developed a more effective system of references to reflect the various relationships between the materials in the canonical Gospels. He divided each Gospel into small, consecutively numbered Sections, apparently providing 355 for Matthew, 233 (241) for Mark,[32] 342 for Luke, and 232 for John. Then he set up ten

[32] When Mark 16:9–20 is included there are 241 Sections.

Canons or Tables to indicate the interrelationships between these Sections. Thus Canon I, which for purposes of arrangement followed the order in Matthew, listed in four columns the material found in all four Gospels. Canons II, III, and IV listed the materials appearing in the various possible combinations of three Gospels, and so on. Finally Canon X, which was divided into four parts, listed the materials unique to each of the Gospels. Eusebius covered every arrangement of the materials that was theoretically possible except Mark-Luke-John and Mark-John. These two were not given separate Canons because there do not seem to be any Sections which appear only in these combinations.

In addition to listing all the Sections in their appropriate Canons at the beginning of the four Gospels, Eusebius also placed beside each Section number in the margin the number of the Canon in which that Section would be found. Thus alongside of Matthew 14:15–21 (the feeding of the five thousand) there appeared the Section number 147 along with the Canon number I. The curious reader could then turn to Canon I—with its four columns—and follow down the Matthew column until he reached the number 147. A quick glance at the parallel columns would give the numbers 64, 93, and 49 respectively, these numbers representing the location of the feeding of the five thousand in the other three Gospels. If the reader remembered the significance of the Canon numbers he would know just by glancing at the margin whether the given narrative had parallels in other Gospels, and, if so, in which Gospels or Gospel. In later centuries it occurred to some scholar that the system would be even more convenient if the Section numbers on the margin of a page were repeated at the bottom of the same page along with the parallels from the other Gospels. Thus it was no longer necessary to look up the Canons at the beginning of the manuscript.

Eusebius' work created a form of "do-it-yourself" harmony. His system told you where to find the parallels, if any, in the other Gospels. However, if an incident occurred in a different

sequence in two or more Gospels you were left to your own in-
genuity to decide which incident to transfer from its original
sequence. But it is noteworthy that Eusebius' arrangement of his
Canons gave a form of priority to the Matthean order. Whether
this expressed a deliberate conviction on the part of Eusebius,
or whether it was due to the pragmatic necessity of having some
order if the Canons were to be of maximum value, is left to our
speculation. His criticism of Ammonius would seem to imply
that he (Eusebius) was unwilling to assume that Matthew's order
was necessarily correct as over against that which might appear
in the other Gospels.

A casual check of the Eusebian system makes it clear that he
felt free to label incidents as parallels even though they occurred
in totally different contexts and with differing detail. In this he
agreed with Tatian. Thus he equated the four stories of the
anointing of Jesus (Matthew 26:6–13; Mark 14:3–9; Luke 7:
36–50; John 12:1–8); the three accounts of the healing of a
Capernaum official's son or servant (Matthew 8:5–13; Luke 7:1–
10; John 4:46–54); the three versions of the dispute about great-
ness (Matthew 20:24–28; Mark 10:41–45; Luke 22:24–27);
the parables of the pounds or talents (Matthew 25:14–30; Luke
19:11–27); the parables of the great supper and the marriage
feast (Matthew 22:1–10; Luke 14:16–24); and the two lamenta-
tions over Jerusalem (Matthew 23:37–39; Luke 13:34–35). On
the other hand, he did not equate the question of the greatest
commandment in Luke 10:25–28 with the similar discussion in
Mark 12:28–31 and Matthew 22:34–40. Many of his identifica-
tions, though not all, correspond with those of Tatian's *Diatessaron,* though there is little reason to assume he was influenced
by this predecessor.

There is a puzzle hidden in the Canons and Sections of Eusebius
which deserves a moment's consideration. The system of Eusebius
has been described as if it constituted a skeleton on which a harmony could be built. More than ninety-five percent of the evi-

dence fits this assumption, and Eusebius' work is generally so reported in the handbooks. But a few features of his arrangement do not fit this purpose. Most perplexing is that the Eusebian Canons equate all three Passovers in John with the final Passover in the Synoptics. Thus John 2:13 (Section 20), John 6:4 (Section 48), and John 11:55 (Section 96) are all listed in Canon I of Eusebius, and their parallels are given as the Passover of passion week. But anyone holding this view must apply some form of "recapitulation" to John's chronology and must assume that the ministry of Jesus was confined to a single year. Now despite the explicit reference to three Passovers in John's Gospel a surprising number of individuals in the early church believed that Jesus' ministry lasted only one year. An examination of Eusebius' other writings reveals that this does not seem to have been his view. Both in the *Chronicles*[33] and in his *Ecclesiastical History*[34] the ministry is portrayed as lasting approximately three years. This question of the Johannine Passovers is only the most puzzling of several peculiarities. According to the Eusebian system the miraculous catch of fish in Luke 5:4–7 (Section 30, Canon IX) is linked with John 21:1–6, 11 (Sections 219, 222, Canon IX), i.e., the post-resurrection catch of fish. Is it really possible that Eusebius carried freedom in rearrangement so far as to identify these two? If so he belonged in the front ranks of modern form critics! Again, the Eusebian system links Matthew 2:5–6 (Herod's informants say the Messiah is to be born in Bethlehem) with John 7:41–42 (another reference to the birth of the Messiah in Bethlehem). Surely Eusebius cannot mean that a reference in the infancy narrative is the same as a reference made during the ministry of Jesus. The number of such passages is not great, but it is sufficient to require explanation.

In the light of these difficulties it was suggested at least as long ago as 1871, in J. W. Burgon's book *The Last Twelve*

---

[33] See the years 2044–2040 after Abraham.
[34] Bk. I, chap. 10, secs. 2 and 6.

Verses of the Gospel of Mark,[35] that Eusebius was not creating a harmony but, rather, a system of marginal references indicating similar though not necessarily identical material. Thus Eusebius could link two discussions concerning the birth of the Messiah in Bethlehem without in any way intending to imply that the two conversations were the same. It is obvious that the bulk of the references would be the same whether they were intended to indicate similar materials or identical materials in different Gospels. Surprisingly the crucial term in Eusebius' *Letter to Carpianus,* namely, *ta paraplēsia,* is ambiguous precisely at this point, and its repetition in the *Letter* does not make it any more explicit.

While the marginal references theory solves the particular difficulties mentioned, is raises a new set: If Eusebius was preparing marginal references, why are so many possible references omitted? Perhaps it can be granted that Eusebius would have found it too complicated to add further Canons indicating "doublets" or similar materials within the same Gospel, but why is Matthew 9:27–31 (healing of two blind men) listed in Canon X as being without parallel when Mark 10:46–52 is at least a similar incident? Or why is Matthew 9:32–34 (healing of a demoniac) not linked with Luke 11:14–15? Or why is Mark 6:14–16 (Elijah *redivivus*) not associated with Luke 9:7–8?

Until further light has been shed on the purpose of Eusebius it will remain uncertain whether he intended to provide a harmony or simply a set of marginal references.[36] If the latter was the case, then his work was not a part of the Quest for the historical Jesus but was merely an aid for preachers who wished to bring together from the four Gospels materials dealing with a

[35] Oxford: Parker, 1871.

[36] A re-examination of the Eusebian system, after the completion of this manuscript, has convinced me that it is misleading to refer to his work as a kind of harmony. It is more accurately described as a primitive system of marginal references. Much of the material may *serve* as a harmony but it distorts the intention of Eusebius to suggest that he intended to answer the question, Where is a given incident in one Gospel reported in the others? See my article "The Eusebian Sections and Canons," *The Catholic Biblical Quarterly,* XXVII (July, 1965), 250–56.

common theme or motif. His work has been considered here, however, on the assumption that, despite certain problems, he did intend to indicate how and where identical incidents were presented in the various Gospels. But Eusebius differed from modern scholars who have charted the same similarities. Apparently Eusebius was content with the knowledge that two or more evangelists had sometimes reported the same saying or incident in almost identical language. He did not ask whether these similarities were so great as to necessitate the assumption the the the evangelists had borrowed from each other or from common written sources. This did not happen until the end of the eighteenth century when more critical methods of source criticism became the fashion both in biblical and secular studies. This critical attitude toward the sources to be used is a characteristic distinction between the earliest and latest phases of the Quest for the historical Jesus.

IV

Augustine was probably the most influential figure in the life of the early church, certainly in the West. Although his genius was more in the area of theological thought than of biblical scholarship, his study *The Harmony of the Gospels* had a profound impact on all subsequent discussion of these problems. Many of the harmonizations which he first proposed continued to be advocated until, in the nineteenth century, a truer understanding of the relationships between the Gospels produced a different approach to these problems. Augustine produced the most detailed study of harmonization in the history of the early or medieval church. He was driven to this laborious task by his awareness that the critics of Christianity were using the alleged discrepancies between the Gospels as a major argument in their critique. In Book I, chapter 7, of the *Harmony* he states: ". . . we must prove that the writers in question do not stand in any antagonism to each other. For those adversaries are in the habit

of adducing this as the palmary allegation in all their vain
objections, namely, that the evangelists are not in harmony with
each other." It was Augustine's intention to silence the critics
outside the church while comforting and reassuring the per-
plexed within. This apologetic concern may sometimes have led
him to regard as probable, conjectures which actually were conceivable but improbable. But this is a distortion which every
scholar risks when he deals with matters which approach the
center of his own convictions, whether those convictions be
negative or affirmative.

In Book I Augustine discusses general matters concerning the
authority, origin, and character of the Gospels. He held the
traditional views concerning their authors and the order of composition. Apparently he assumed that the later evangelists were
familiar with the work of their predecessors, but he does not
suggest that they borrowed directly from the earlier. It is often
stated that Augustine regarded Mark as an abbreviated version
of Matthew, but his actual language may mean only that Mark
gives the impression of being an "epitome" of Matthew. He may
not have intended to imply that Mark actually originated in this
fashion.[37] Augustine also discussed the relation of the Synoptics
to John, concluding that the former were concerned primarily
with the humanity of Jesus while John was concerned with the
divinity. He suggested further that the Synoptics were intended
to encourage the "active" virtues, but John the "contemplative."

In Book II Augustine began the actual discussion of apparent
discrepancies. He followed the order of Matthew, dealing with
difficulties of order or phraseology arising when the material
of this Gospel is compared with that in the others. Book II followed this pattern up to the Lord's Supper in Matthew 26, while
Book III presented the subsequent events in a unified narrative
but with discussion of apparent discrepancies. In Book IV he

[37] See Bk. I, chap. 2.

retraced his steps to consider miscellaneous narratives in Mark, Luke, or John which had been omitted because the outline of Matthew had been followed.

How did Augustine deal with the variations of order or phraseology in the four Gospels? On the one hand he was committed to a high view of inspiration and insisted that the veracity of each evangelist must be defended.

> It is only seemly that no charge of absolute unveracity should be laid against the Evangelists, and that, too, not only with regard to that kind of unveracity which comes by positive telling of what is false, but also with regard to that which arises through forgetfulness. . . .[38]

On the other hand Augustine achieved a degree of flexibility in handling the materials by contending (a) that the order of events in the Gospels was sometimes the order of recollection rather than the order of history;[39] (b) that when the Gospels reported conversations it was adequate for them to report the sense intended rather than the precise words; and (c) that since any one Gospel generally reported only part of an event, varying details in other Gospels should be regarded as supplementary and not contradictory.

While this recognition of variations between the Gospels in matters of order or detail reflected a valid historical sense on Augustine's part it created something of a theological problem for him, since he was prepared to insist that in the case of the evangelists even the accidents of memory were controlled by the Holy Spirit. But there is some inconsistency in explaining discrepancies by appeal to the accidents of memory if one also argues that the Holy Spirit has controlled the accidents. In Book II, chapter 12, he quoted some who felt that the Holy Spirit should have guided the evangelists so as to "secure them against all variation the one from the other, either in the kind of words,

---

[38] Bk. II, chap. 12.
[39] See above, p. 12.

or in their order, or in their number. . . ." He replied that these individuals should recognize that the policy followed by the Holy Spirit had served the useful purpose of demonstrating that witnesses may be reliable without being in complete verbal agreement. It is possible that Augustine was not wholly satisfied with this response. At any rate he raised the question again and stated that it is a "question which any one may look into with pious consideration, and for which, by divine help, the answer also may be found. That, however, is not the object of the work which we have taken in hand at present."[40] This leaves the question rather up in the air! Elsewhere Augustine argued also that the variations between the evangelists helped to bring out the full meaning which, presumably, would not have been clear had the testimony of a single evangelist been taken by itself.

Another principle Augustine was at pains to stress was that apparent doublets may represent different events since Jesus undoubtedly repeated much of his teaching several times over and since what happened once in his ministry may have happened again. Following this principle Augustine argued for, or assumed, two cleansings of the temple,[41] two healings of a Capernaum official's son or servant,[42] two discussions about the great commandment,[43] two parables of the marriage feast or great feast,[44] two anointings at Bethany,[45] and, probably, two Sermons on the Mount (Plain).[46] An extreme illustration of this principle is to be found in his handling of the healings near Jericho. Augustine was able to equate the Matthean and Marcan versions even though Matthew speaks of two blind men and Mark only of one. But he did not feel free to identify the Lucan version with the other two since Luke placed the incident *before*

[40] Bk. II, chap. 21.
[41] Bk. II, chap. 67.
[42] Bk. II, chap. 20; and Bk. IV, chap. 10.
[43] Bk. III, chap. 73.
[44] Bk. II, chap. 71.
[45] Bk. II, chap. 79.
[46] Bk. II, chap. 19.

Jesus' entry into Jericho while Matthew and Mark placed it after his departure. Clearly Augustine was prepared to rearrange the order of the Gospels, but he was reluctant to do so against their explicit statements of time or relationship. A similar duplication of incidents occurs in his handling of the prediction of Peter's denial of Jesus.[47] Here Augustine felt compelled to posit three separate predictions in order to avoid any clash of details. On other occasions he shifted and combined incidents with comparative freedom, e.g., the equation of Matthew 8:18–22 (the would-be disciples) with Luke 9:57–60, or his identification of the rejection at Nazareth as reported by Luke with that in the other two Synoptics.

Augustine was acutely conscious of the problems of harmonization, but occasionally one cannot escape the impression that he was compelled to engage in special pleading in order to maintain his views. For example, there is his attempt to harmonize the injunction not to take a "staff" in Matthew 10:10 (Luke 9:3) with the apparently contradictory command in Mark 6:8.[48] It is valid to argue that the same term may be used with different meanings in different contexts, but the application of the principle in this instance appears forced. Another instance is found in Book II, chapter 78, where Augustine dealt with the apparent chronological discrepancies of the anointing at Bethany as recorded in John 12:1 and in Matthew 26:1–13. A further illustration of strained exegesis is in Book III, chapter 2, where he attempted to harmonize the verbal details of Mark 14:30 ("before the cock crows twice") and Matthew 26:34 ("before the cock crows"). Augustine's basic principle was sensible and consistent, namely, that the evangelists agreed in substance but not necessarily in detail. However, his application of this principle was sometimes weak and inconsistent because he was reluctant to admit any direct or explicit contradiction even in matters

[47] Bk. III, chap. 2.
[48] Bk. II, chap. 30.

of detail. It is now clear (for example, from Matthew's revision of Mark) that the evangelists were simply not interested in accuracy of detail.

In general, Augustine's handling of harmonization problems was more "conservative" than that of Tatian or Eusebius; this was unfortunate for the subsequent development of the discussion. He was less free in the rearrangement of order and in the identification of incidents despite discrepant details, though he would have been completely baffled by the far more extreme views of Andreas Osiander and some other sixteenth-century Protestant harmonists.[49] The basic arrangement of his discussion favored the outline of Matthew, though he felt free to adopt the chronology of the other Gospels. In the area of Gospel studies, as in so many others, his influence was enormous, and many of his suggestions were repeated for centuries, for example, in sixteenth- and seventeenth-century Gospel harmonies.[50]

This chapter has dealt with two movements in the early church, both of which were related to the Quest for the historical Jesus.[51] First, the establishment of the four Gospels—Matthew, Mark, Luke, and John—as the authoritative sources for the portrayal of the ministry of Jesus. Second, the efforts to combine this four-fold tradition into a unified "Life" of Jesus. From the perspec-

[49] See below, pp. 83 ff.

[50] This was true of his phraseology distinguishing between "the order of recollection" and "the order of occurrence." It is also true of his reference to events narrated "by anticipation," by which Augustine meant that, in his judgment, the evangelist placed these events prior to their historical order of occurrence. (Later writers also employed his phrase "by recapitulation" to designate an event presented by an evangelist at some point later than its probable historical occurrence.) See Bk. II, chaps. 31, 32, 34, 44, 48, 78; Bk. III, chap. 2. Or, to take an example of a specific harmonization that influenced generations of interpreters, note his contention in Bk. II, chap. 65, that Mark 10:46 mentions only one blind man (i.e., Bartimaeus), because he was the more famous of the two referred to in Matt. 20:30. Augustine used the same explanation in connection with the similar discrepancy between Matt. 8:28 and Mark 5:2.

[51] Other evidence of an early interest in the historical Jesus is discussed in Robert M. Grant's study *The Earliest Lives of Jesus* (New York: Harper, 1961), which deals particularly with Clement and Origen of Alexandria.

tive of modern scholarship the first of these movements achieved a remarkable success, but the effort to harmonize the four Gospels failed to reach any satisfactory conclusion. The work of Tatian, Eusebius, Augustine, and others, involved experimentation with various possibilities; without this experimentation subsequent developments might have been impossible. But no satisfactory solution was possible until it was recognized that the four evangelists were *not* independent sources presenting essentially eyewitness material. Without this insight the Gospels could continue to fulfill their function as witnesses to the apostolic faith which arose in response to the life and ministry of Jesus, but the misunderstanding concerning their origins and nature obscured the problems which stimulated the modern version of the Quest for the historical Jesus. Despite Augustine's assumption that the later evangelists knew the work of their predecessors, no scholar until the modern period recognized that the Gospels were in some way dependent one on the other. This discovery, and its implications, opened a fruitful period of scholarship but also created false illusions and false fears. This story is the subject matter for chapter five.

3

The *Vitae Christi* of the Fourteenth Century

The previous chapter pointed out that the Quest began in the earliest Christian centuries as the church sought to determine which Gospels should be regarded as authoritative and as it attempted to combine these Gospels into some form of unified harmony.[1] Throughout the patristic and medieval periods the literature produced by the Quest was comparatively limited. For those familiar with the academic discussions concerning the "Life" of Jesus during the nineteenth and twentieth centuries it is surprising to discover that when Friedrich Schleiermacher began his lectures on "The Life of Jesus" in 1819 at the recently founded University of Berlin his subject was regarded as an innovation in the University curriculum.[2] An even greater surprise awaits the researcher who examines the nearly four hundred volumes of Migne's *Patrologia Latina* and *Patrologia Graeca*.[3] Although these volumes contain the works of the major Christian

---

[1] Admittedly the preservation of oral tradition about Jesus, and then the writing down of that tradition, was the earliest version of the Quest. However, the story, insofar as it can be known, is too well-known to need repetition here.

[2] Friedrich Schleiermacher, *Das Leben Jesu* (*Sämmtliche Werke,* Vol. VI; Berlin: George Reimer, 1864).

[3] *Patrologia Latina,* ed. J. P. Migne (221 vols.; Paris, 1844 ff.) ; *Patrologia Graeca,* ed. J. P. Migne (162 vols.; Paris, 1857 ff.).

writers down to the thirteenth and fifteenth centuries respectively, they do not include any writing which by strict definition could be called a "Life of Christ." Before turning to the *Vitae Christi* which appeared in the fourteenth century it may be helpful to indicate certain other types of literature which were produced and which were at least related to the Quest.[4]

I

Certainly the apocryphal gospels which have appeared in every century, but which were especially numerous in the early Christian centuries, stand in some relationship to the Quest for the historical Jesus. Yet they are scarcely in a direct line with that Quest. With a little oversimplification these apocryphal gospels may be divided into two groups: those with a primarily doctrinal or theological interest and those with a predominantly historical interest. Most of the Gnostic gospels belong in the first category, and the so-called Gospel of Truth recently discovered at Chenoboskion is an outstanding example of a pure form of this category.[5] In fact it is so exclusively theological in its interests that it is not truly a gospel in the usual sense of that term. On the other hand the Gospel of Thomas, which deals with the boyhood of Jesus, is a pure form of the historical type.[6] That the events narrated are based on pious imagination rather than on serious historical evidence does not alter the fact that this work seeks to present an aspect of the life of the historical Jesus. It was a characteristic of apocryphal gospels of the historical type that they concentrated on a single period in the life of Jesus rather than on his life as a whole. Two periods in the life of Jesus were of special interest to the creators of this literature: the birth

[4] In this connection consideration should be given to the commentaries on the Gospels, but the subject is too broad for cursory summary, and we shall have to pass over this strand of the interest in the historical Jesus.

[5] *Evangelium Veritatis,* ed. Michel Malinine, Henri-Charles Puech, Gilles Quispel (Zurich: Rascher, 1956).

[6] See "The Gospel of Thomas" in M. R. James, *The Apocryphal New Testament* (Oxford: Clarendon, 1950 reprinting), pp. 49–68. This gospel is not to be confused with the recently discovered Coptic, Gnostic gospel of the same name.

and boyhood of Jesus or, alternatively, the story of his sufferings and resurrection. If the Gospel of Thomas illustrates the former interest, the Gospel of Peter demonstrates the latter with its retelling of the trial and crucifixion of Jesus.[7] Conceivably some of the earliest apocryphal gospels may have attempted to portray the entire life of Jesus, but since they are known to us only in fragments it is precarious to speak too confidently concerning them.

It is likely that the apocryphal gospels of the historical type appearing in the second century retained some link with the historical Jesus, but those of the later periods became increasingly detached from historical reality. While they reflect an interest in the historical Jesus they lack the critical faculty essential for the successful implementation of that interest. Since the major leaders of the church concurred in the establishment of the four canonical Gospels as authoritative and viewed the others with greater or lesser suspicion, it is probable that the continued production and circulation of apocryphal gospels reflected the activity of the lower levels in the life of the church. These productions belonged to folk literature, and this genre could not be expected to make much contribution to the Quest for the historical Jesus.

During the fourth and fifth centuries a different form of literature appeared dealing with the life of Jesus, namely, the poetic presentations of his career. These were in Latin, confined themselves chiefly to the materials in the canonical Gospels (especially Matthew), and reflect a dependence on Virgil. (The influence of Virgil during this period is indicated by the large number of manuscripts of his writings still extant from the third to the fifth centuries.) In a sense these works were Gospel harmonies in poetry, although the authors exercised considerable poetic license since they omitted substantial blocks of the Gospel ma-

[7] See "The Gospel of Peter" in Edgar Hennecke-Wilhelm Schneemelcher, *New Testament Apocrypha,* Vol. I (Philadelphia: Westminster, 1963), pp. 179–87.

terial and, following a general tendency of the early church, placed chief reliance on Matthew. Although these documents reflect an interest in the historical figure of Jesus, there is no evidence that their authors were conscious of any need for a Quest in order to discover that figure. Like the Gospel harmonists they took for granted the authoritative character of the four accepted Gospels, and their sole concern was to present this known figure to their readers in poetic form. Their interest was in teaching and not in research. It is possible that these early "Lives" appeared in poetry because prose "Lives" would have seemed redundant since prose gospels already existed.[8]

One of the earliest of these works was the *Evangeliorum Libri Quattuor* of the Spanish presbyter, Juvencus, written about A.D. 330.[9] It was divided into four books with a total of over 3,200 lines. The Gospel tradition was followed comparatively closely with special attention being paid to Matthew. The author attempted to present the Christian story as an epic in Virgilian style. Jerome commented that Juvencus "did not shrink from forcing into metre the majestic phrases of the Gospel."[10] There is a degree of monotony in the style, but this did not keep the work from being widely read for many centuries.

Less successful from a literary standpoint was the *Cento,* written about the middle of the fourth century by Proba, a woman from a distinguished patrician family of Rome.[11] The entire work has only 694 hexameter lines, and nearly half of these form a prologue dealing with the beginnings of the biblical tradition, especially Genesis 1–3. Thus the actual story of Christ's life is greatly compressed, and, as was the custom, major attention was

---

[8] However, one of the authors, Sedulius, followed his writing of a poetic life, the *Carmen Paschale,* with a supplementary work in prose entitled the *Opus Paschale.*

[9] See *Corpus Scriptorum Ecclesiasticorum Latinorum,* Vol. XXIV, ed. Johannes Huemer (Vienna, 1891).

[10] Jerome, Letter 70:5. The quotation is from the translation by W. H. Freemantle, *The Nicene and Post-Nicene Fathers,* Second Series, ed. Philip Schaff and Henry Wace, Vol. VI (New York, 1893; reprinted, Eerdmans, 1954), p. 151.

[11] See *Corpus Scriptorum Ecclesiasticorum Latinorum,* Vol. XVI, ed. C. Schenkl (Vienna, 1888).

devoted to the beginning and the end of the life. However, other material is presented, for example, the Sermon on the Mount in lines 467–494. Presumably Proba was a convert to Christianity, and her poem reflects the enthusiasm of the convert rather than any distinctive genius in the field of Virgilian poetry. Yet the document had some popularity and consequently found its way into the long list of apocryphal writings cited in the *Decretum Gelasianum* as being without the approval of the Roman church.[12]

A third work of this type was the *Carmen Paschale* of the fifth-century Italian poet, Sedulius.[13] The first of the poem's five Books deals with the Old Testament prologue to the Gospel story, while the remaining four Books portray the birth, life, death, and resurrection of Christ. Unlike the poems of Juvencus or Proba the *Carmen Paschale* does not merely repeat the Gospel narrative but adds reflections and comments on its meaning. Sedulius had more originality than either of his predecessors and his work was popular for a number of centuries. Probably the allegorical or symbolic interpretations which he occasionally presented increased the popularity of his work.[14]

Since Latin was not the language of the common people, there was need for "Lives" of Jesus in the vernacular. In part this was met by translations from the Latin and in part by original creations in the vernacular languages, although even these latter were often partially dependent on earlier Latin works such as the Latin translation(s) of Tatian's *Diatessaron*. Notable illustrations of this vernacular literature are the ninth-century Old Saxon documents, the *Heliand*[15] and Otfrid's *Evangelienbuch*.[16] If the Prologue now attached to the first of these is

[12] Hennecke-Schneemelcher, *op. cit.,* I, 46–49.
[13] See *Corpus Scriptorum Ecclesiasticorum Latinorum,* Vol. X, ed. Johannes Huemer (Vienna, 1885).
[14] For example, his suggestion that the four evangelists correspond to the four seasons, or his suggestion that the four arms of the cross indicate the four cardinal points.
[15] *Heliand und Genesis,* ed. Walter Mitzka ("Altdeutsche Textbibliothek," No. 4, 7th ed.; Tübingen: Max Niemeyer, 1958).
[16] *Otfrids Evangelienbuch,* ed. Ludwig Wolff ("Altdeutsche Textbibliothek," No. 49, 3rd ed.; Tübingen: Max Niemeyer, 1957).

accurate, the poem was prepared at the request of Louis the Pious (d. A.D. 840) for the instruction of his Saxon subjects who had been converted to Christianity in a somewhat ruthless fashion. The author followed the outline of the *Diatessaron* which he knew in a Latin form, but his work reflects an acquaintance also with the commentaries widely used in his day, e.g., Rhabanus Maurus on Matthew, Bede on Mark and Luke, and Alcuin on John.[17] The author's knowledge of current theological thought suggests that he had been trained in this field, but some critics of his work feel that the "this-worldly" vigor of his poetry indicates a more secular background.

Otfrid, the author of the *Evangelienbuch,* was a monk from the monastery of Weissenburg in Alsace. Writing about A.D. 868 it was his deliberate intention, as he stated in the opening pages, to replace the popular, secular songs of his day with religious poetry presenting the life of Christ. The poetic narrative is interspersed with digressions as Otfrid repeatedly turned aside to elaborate the moral or spiritual meaning of a particular passage.[18]

Both of these writings were widely read in the subsequent centuries and were significant in the developing history of German literature as well as in the religious sphere. However, like the other poetic presentations of the life of Christ, they reflect no interest in a Quest, since they were built on the assumption that in the four Gospels the life of Jesus is fully and accurately known. This assumption did not prevent the admixture of some apocryphal details, but these served as a form of pious embroidery around the edges of the completed cloth of the canonical Gospels.

Despite the predominance of the theological and doctrinal interest, or perhaps alongside of this interest, there continued through the centuries a genuine concern with the actual life and humanity of Jesus. This concern was fostered by some of the

---

[17] See the Mitzka ed. of *Heliand und Genesis,* pp. xxvii–xxviii.
[18] See Bk. I, chaps. 26, 28, and Bk. II, chaps. 5, 9, *et al.*

religious orders, for example, the Cistercians,[19] and, later, the Franciscans.[20] It was this interest which found expression, particularly in the fourteenth century, in what are known as the *Vitae Christi.* Three of these will be considered in this chapter: *The Meditations on the Life of Christ,* the *De Gestis Domini Salvatoris,* and the *Vita Christi.*

II

For several centuries it was assumed that *The Meditations on the Life of Christ* was the work of Bonaventure, the Italian, Franciscan theologian who died in 1274. It is now agreed that the author was an unknown Franciscan who wrote at the end of the thirteenth or the beginning of the fourteenth century and is now referred to as Pseudo-Bonaventure. Originally written as a devotional guide for a nun, the book became immensely popular, being translated into various languages and appearing in a number of editions. Over two hundred Latin, Italian, and French manuscripts are still extant as evidence of its widespread popularity.[21] The most complete English translation, and that quoted in this study, is by Isa Ragusa and Rosalie B. Green and is based on the fourteenth-century Italian Manuscript 115 in the Bibliothèque Nationale in Paris.[22] Since the Italian manuscript is broken off at the end, the translators used the standard Latin edition for the concluding quarter of the text.

[19] Founded in 1098 at Citeaux by Robert of Molesme.

[20] Founded in 1209 by Francis of Assisi.

[21] For the Latin text see *Bonaventurae Opera Omnia,* Vol. XII, ed. A. C. Peltier (Paris, 1868).

[22] *Meditations on the Life of Christ* (Princeton: Princeton University Press, 1961; the quotations in the text are used by permission of the publisher). The manuscript on which this translation was based is noteworthy in that it contains the "long" text rather than one of the numerous abbreviations, and also because of the large number of illustrations which it includes. There are nearly two hundred illustrations in the manuscript; these are reproduced in the Ragusa-Green translation. Spaces (and instructions for filling them) were left for an additional hundred illustrations. Since the missing quarter must also have had space for further illustrations, the manuscript as originally projected must have been prepared for some four hundred illustrations. There are other English translations, e.g., that of Sister M. Emmanuel, O.S.B., *Meditations on the Life of Christ* (St. Louis and London: Herder, 1934).

As the title implies the work is a series of *meditations* on the life of Christ rather than a "Life" in the strict sense of that term. But in the tradition of the Cistercians and Franciscans such meditations proceeded on the basis of an imaginative recapitulation of the actual scenes in the life of Christ. Since the goal was imaginative and devotional participation in the events themselves, the achievement of this goal required the reconstruction of the original scenes. When the meditations followed the chronological pattern of the Gospels—as in this work—the result was a devotional study built on the foundation of a "Life" of Christ.

The Prologue begins:

> Among the noteworthy virtues and excellences of the most holy Saint Cecilia, we read that she always carried the Gospel of Christ hidden in her bosom, which I think means that she had chosen the most pious facts of the life of Jesus, as shown in the Gospels, on which to meditate day and night with pure and undivided heart and singleminded and fervent intent. . . . I wish to encourage you to do likewise because, above all the studies of spiritual exercise, I believe that this one is the most necessary and the most fruitful and the one that may lead to the highest level. You will never find better instruction against vain and fleeting blandishments, against tribulation and adversity, against the temptations of enemies and vices, than in the life of Christ, which was without blemish and most perfect. Through frequent and continued meditation on His life the soul attains so much familiarity, confidence, and love that it will disdain and disregard other things and be exercised and trained as to what to do and what to avoid.[23]

Similarly in the extended discussion of the active and contemplative life which is attached to the Mary and Martha incident,[24] the author discusses the higher forms of contemplation but then warns the reader that the gateway to all contemplation is medita-

[23] *Ibid.*, p. 1.
[24] See chaps. 45–58 (*ibid.*, pp. 245–90). This is the longest discussion of a single theme in the entire book and reflects a basic medieval interest. Yet there are numerous manuscripts without these chapters, which definitely retard the narrative.

tion "on the humanity of Christ." This is not only the initial and basic form of contemplation but it is also the form which accompanies the first stage of the active life which, according to the author, precedes general contemplation by way of preparation and purification. He quotes Bernard on this form of contemplation and then terminates his quotation with the comment that he need not continue it since actually his entire book is a contemplation of the humanity of Christ.

It is in accord with this purpose that the author constantly exhorts the reader to relive the events of Jesus' life and ministry. Frequently the narrative shifts into the present tense as the reader is exhorted to "watch," "see," "accompany," or "follow" the actions and experiences of Christ. It is significant that the longer Gospel speeches, such as the Sermon on the Mount and the discourses in John 14–17, are almost entirely ignored since the author preferred to recapitulate the dramatic scenes of things that happened, these having more power to draw the reader into the events as a participant. Admittedly the extended quotations, chiefly from Bernard, tend to weaken this dramatic effect. Perhaps the writer was aware of this difficulty since, when he reaches the passion narrative, he states that he will omit quotations in order to allow the reader to concentrate on the events themselves.[25] Having completed the passion narrative he compensates for these omissions by quoting in succession a series of comments from Bernard.[26]

Despite the predominance of the devotional interest the work provides a "Life" of Christ. This is because the author maintains a relatively consistent adherence to the chronology of the Gospels. It is not apparent that he took any one Gospel as his basic guide, and it is unlikely that he troubled himself much about the original, historical order. He seems to have assumed that incidents appearing in different contexts in two or more

[25] See chap. 64 (p. 297).
[26] See chap. 85 (p. 351).

Gospels were separate incidents no matter how similar the details may have been. Thus he differentiates the Johannine from the Synoptic cleansing of the temple, the calling of disciples in Luke 5:1–11 from that in Mark 1:16–20 (Matt. 4:18–22), the healing of the blind beggar in Luke 18:35–43 from that in Mark 10:46–52 (Matt. 20:29–34), and the healing of a nobleman's son in John 4:46–54 from the similar incident in Matthew 8:5–13 and Luke 7:1–10. However, while stating that these are distinct incidents he discusses them together, presumably because a meditation on one would be equally appropriate for the similar incident. Obviously, this procedure resulted in dislocations of the order found in one or more of the Gospels.

Furthermore, an unusual dislocation of the Gospel order occurs in connection with the passion narrative. The author states that after describing the arrival of Jesus in Jerusalem he intends to focus attention solely on the "Supper" and the "Passion."[27] In order to achieve this objective he will deal in advance with some events which happened during the Jerusalem ministry. In this context he refers specifically to his handling of the cursing of the fig tree and the woman taken in adultery; but the same logic probably explains his having discussed still earlier the temple cleansing,[28] the question of tribute,[29] and the parable of the wicked tenants.[30] Another dislocation occurs in chapter 38 where he combines various incidents in which critics of Jesus are reported to have been scandalized at his words (Matt. 15:1–14; Mark 7:1–13; John 6:52–59; Luke 11:37–53).

The author's concern to identify his sources is another indication that, although the *Meditations* is primarily a devotional guide, it is at least secondarily a "Life" of Jesus. Obviously, the author did not evaluate his sources according to the norms of a nineteenth- or twentieth-century scholar, but he did provide

---

[27] Chap. 67 (p. 301).
[28] Chap. 42 (p. 229).
[29] Chap. 60 (p. 291).
[30] Chap. 59 (pp. 290 f.).

the reader with the information necessary to allow him to check on the author's sources. This is the more surprising since he warned the reader in the Prologue that not everything which he reports must be taken as pure history.

> . . . However, you must not believe that all things said and done by Him on which we may meditate are known to us in writing. For the sake of greater impressiveness I shall tell them to you as they occurred *or as they might have occurred according to the devout belief of the imagination and the varying interpretation of the mind.* . . . Thus when you find it said here, "This was said and done by the Lord Jesus," and by others of whom we read, if it cannot be demonstrated by the Scriptures, you must consider it only as a requirement of devout contemplation. Take it as if I had said, "Suppose that this is what the Lord Jesus said and did," and also for similar things.[31]

From these remarks it might be expected that the author would use his pious imagination rather freely, but this does not prove to be the case. It is likely that the words in the Prologue are intended to indicate the author's plan to use traditional materials from outside the Scriptures rather than as a justification for the use of his own imagination. This is confirmed by a subsequent comment: "I do not intend to affirm anything in this little book that is not asserted or said by Holy Scripture *or the word of the saints or by approved opinion.*"[32]

Not only does the author confine his extra-canonical remarks to established tradition, he also indicates when he has moved from Scripture to tradition and frequently identifies the source of the tradition.[33] Thus he refers to the *Historia Scholastica* of Peter Comestor to support the view that the wedding at Cana was that of John the Evangelist;[34] he uses the same work as a source for

---

[31] Page 5 (italics added). See also chaps. 9 and 15.
[32] Chap. 74 (p. 318; italics added).
[33] The term "tradition" is used rather loosely in this context.
[34] Chap. 20 (p. 140).

his comment on the column to which Jesus was tied for flogging[35] and in support of the claim that the cross was fifteen feet high.[36] He cites the Gospel of Nicodemus as his authority for the resurrection appearance to Joseph of Arimathea.[37] The *Glossa Ordinaria* is cited on several occasions, for example, when the author describes Jesus' "passing through the midst of" the Nazareth mob as an escape made possible by a ledge of rock,[38] or when he says that it was the sins of the accusers which Jesus wrote in the sand in connection with the story of the woman taken in adultery.[39] He repeatedly indicates the distances between points in Palestine, and in chapter 17 states that he had learned these from those who had visited the area.[40] After describing the appearance of the resurrected Christ to Mary he states that this is not mentioned in the Gospels but that he has included it because "the Church seems to hold to it, as it is more fully given in the legend of the Resurrection."[41] Presumably the reference is to the *Golden Legend* of Jacobus a Voragine. Similarly he refers one or more times to Augustine, Jerome, Bede, and Martial. On a few occasions he implies that a source has been used but does not supply its name, for example, when identifying the blind man of John 9 as "Celidonius,"[42] when explaining the Gethsemene prayer,[43] or when referring to the tradition that the head of Jesus was shaved and his beard torn.[44] In isolated cases he refers to information received from a contemporary who, ap-

[35] Chap. 76 (p. 329).
[36] Chap. 77 (p. 331).
[37] Chap. 96 (p. 373).
[38] Chap. 32 (p. 193).
[39] Chap. 68 (p. 302).
[40] Pilgrimages to the Holy Land began at least as early as the fourth century. This activity was stimulated by the crusades. A few of these pilgrims published their travel diaries. For translations of a number of these see the volumes published by The Palestine Pilgrims' Text Society, London; for example, *Ludolph von Suchem's Description of the Holy Land,* trans. Aubrey Stewart (London: The Palestine Pilgrims' Text Society, 1896).
[41] Chap. 89 (p. 365).
[42] Chap. 63 (p. 296).
[43] Chap. 75 (p. 324).
[44] Chap. 82 (p. 342).

parently, claimed to have obtained it by revelation.[45] Finally a few extrabiblical incidents are introduced without any hint as to their source. Thus he records a conversation of Jesus with his mother and Mary Magdalene concerning his death and the coming Passover. This is introduced with the words, "Here one may interpolate a very beautiful meditation of which the Scripture does not speak."[46] Again there are extended descriptions of the placing of Jesus on the cross and, later, of his removal.[47] In connection with the details of the nailing to the cross he states that there is an alternative view current and then adds an appropriate meditation for anyone accepting this alternative view. Presumably all such items were taken from current tradition and were not the products of the author's private reconstruction of the history.

Occasionally the author engaged in a bit of historical analysis in order to support a conclusion not explicit in the text of Scripture itself. A clear example of this is in his account of the wedding at Cana, in which he presents a variety of ingenious arguments to prove that Mary was present at the wedding not as a guest but as the "director and mistress of the wedding."[48] In chapter 15 he analyzes the silence of Scripture concerning the activities of Jesus from his twelfth to his twenty-ninth year and concludes that Jesus did nothing notable during this period.[49]

While the *Meditations* approximate a "Life" of Christ, in the broad sense of the term, they do not utilize all of the available Gospel material. Caprice and the special interests of the author may have played some role in the omissions; but two principles are clear both from an examination of the omitted materials and from the author's own remarks. Chapter 18 deals with the be-

[45] Chaps. 7 and 8 (pp. 32 and 43 ff.).
[46] Chap. 72 (pp. 308 ff.).
[47] Chap. 78 (pp. 333 f.) and chap. 81 (p. 341). The relevant section in the former reference begins, "Here pay diligent attention to the manner of the Crucifixion. Two ladders are set in place. . . ."
[48] Chap. 20 (pp. 140 ff.).
[49] Chap. 15 (pp. 96 f.).

ginning of Jesus' ministry after the baptism and temptation. At this point the author says:

> By the grace of God we have up to here traced the life of the Lord Jesus in orderly fashion, leaving out little or almost nothing of what happened to Him or what He did. But it is not my intention to do this from here on, for it would take too long to convert into meditations all the things He said and did. . . . Therefore we shall choose a few things, on which we intend to meditate continually, from here to the Passion, and beyond that we must not omit anything.[50]

This illustrates the first principle governing the omissions, namely, that the infancy and passion narratives should be treated fully, but the intervening ministry only selectively. In taking this position the author was following a general tendency of the Middle Ages, a tendency which was only gradually overcome as full scale "Lives" began to be written.

A second principle is apparent as soon as the omissions in the *Meditations* are charted. The Gospel chapters omitted either entirely or in large part are Matthew 5–7, 10, 13, 18, 23–25; Mark 4, 13; Luke 10–17; John 3, 7, 14–17. Since these are precisely the chapters containing the major discourses of Jesus, it is obvious that the author of the *Meditations* chose to present incidents rather than speeches. Chapter 21 deals briefly with the opening sections of the Sermon on the Mount, and then contains the rather surprising observation:

> Read it often and diligently and commit to memory the things said in it, for they are spiritual. But now I will not continue in this, for it would take too long *and these expositions do not always seem to benefit meditations,* although I shall intersperse such moral facts and sayings of saints for your instruction as occur to me.[51]

Presumably the author felt the same way about the other discourses which he omitted. His major interest was in the dramatic

[50] Chap. 18 (p. 133).
[51] Chap. 21 (p. 152; italics added).

scenes of the incidents so vividly portrayed in the pages of the Gospels.

Although the *Meditations* is primarily a devotional study and not a "Life" of Jesus, insofar as it is a "Life" how does it compare with modern "Lives"? Certain striking differences are immediately apparent.

First, the author of the *Meditations* is totally confident of the accuracy of his sources and feels no need to probe behind them. This confidence affected not only his use of the Gospels but also his use of the Fathers and the more widely used apocryphal literature. Because of this confidence the author had no consciousness of a "Quest" in the modern sense. His task was to arrange the facts, not to discover them. He was not wrestling with the problem of his sources but with the problem of making spiritually meaningful the truth manifestly present in those sources.

Second, the author had no interest in the question of the internal or external development of the ministry of Jesus. Theological presuppositions may explain his disinterest in the question of development in the thought of Jesus himself. While the author was concerned with the human experiences of Jesus, he never forgot that he was dealing with one who was divine in his inner consciousness. The traditional formulation of this doctrine did not allow much room for such development. In chapter 8 it is recorded that the human Jesus, when he was eight days old, wept because of the pain involved in circumcision; but when his mother wept he immediately stopped his weeping to comfort his mother. Such divine precocity excludes the possibility of genuine development. But neither does the *Meditations* reflect interest in the development of the external ministry of Jesus. The author was little concerned with the changes which may have occurred in the responses either of those who opposed or those who supported Jesus. In fact, the stress on "development" is a characteristic of the modern age.

Third, the author's certainty that the *significance* of Christ was fully revealed in the tradition made him free to use historical details to illustrate that significance without concern for their literal accuracy. Where the significance of the "Life" is fully known, the historical details are merely instruments to bring out that meaning; and the meaning itself is not changed by the conclusion that one set of historical details is accurate or inaccurate.

The differences between the fourteenth and the twentieth centuries are so great that it is difficult to evaluate the *Meditations*. Yet in its day it was clearly a moving and effective document. Even in our times he who reads with sympathy is aware of its power. The digressions may occasionally go too far afield—notably in the prolonged discussion of the active and contemplative lives in connection with the Mary-Martha incident.[52] Or, occasionally, the interpretation may distort the original significance of an incident—as in the discussion of gluttony and abstinence in connection with the story of plucking grain on the Sabbath.[53] But, in the main, this is an effective presentation of the life of Jesus with special reference to the Franciscan virtues of poverty and humility.

III

Simone Fidati, a member of the Order of Hermits of St. Augustine, was the author of a life of Jesus commonly known as the *De Gestis Domini Salvatoris*. Fidati was born about 1300 at Cascia in central Italy. He began his studies in the field of "natural science," but before having proceeded very far he turned to theology after an encounter with "a man who had a reputation for living a holy life."[54] It is generally agreed that Angelo of

---

[52] Chaps. 45–58 (pp. 245–90).

[53] Chap. 44 (p. 233).

[54] The phrase is from Fidati's own biographical note in Bk. VIII, chap. 40, and is quoted from Sister Mary Germaine McNeil's study, *Simone Fidati and his De Gestis Domini Salvatoris* (Washington: The Catholic University of America Press, 1950), pp. 7 f. This study provides an excellent introduction to Fidati and is referred to frequently in the pages which follow. For a biography see also Nicola Mattiola, *Il Beato Simone Fidati de Cascia* (Rome: Antologia Agostiniana, 2, 1898).

Clareno, a Franciscan Spiritual, was the person most influential
in Fidati's later religious life, though it is not quite certain that
he was the one who first turned Fidati's attention to theology.
Angelo represented the radical wing of the Franciscans, i.e.,
those who found themselves in difficulties because of their rigorous
emphasis on the total poverty of Jesus. This stress on poverty and
austerity is reflected in Fidati, although the joyousness which
frequently characterized the radical Franciscans was not equally
apparent in his writings.

Fidati became noted as a preacher and pastoral counsellor.
According to John of Salerno, his disciple and biographer, he
sometimes wrote thirty or forty letters in a single night, continuing with his writing until morning. His homiletic and pastoral
interests found expression in his major writings, the *Vita Christiana* and *De Gestis Domini Salvatoris*. The former was written as
a popular work in 1333 while Fidati was preaching in Florence.
The *De Gestis,* begun at the urging of his influential friend, the
Florentine lawyer Thomas Corsini, was written during the decade
1338–48 and was still incomplete at Fidati's death in 1348. The
bulk of the material was in penultimate form and it was prepared for publication by John of Salerno. The latter doubtless
followed the pattern which Fidati had outlined in the second
of his two Prologues. However, this Prologue gives *De fine
hominum* as the title of the final Book. Since no such Book appears in the manuscripts or the published versions of the *De
Gestis,* it is likely that John, finding no adequate materials left for
this theme, substituted a treatise which Fidati had written earlier,
De justicia christiani. Some years later John published an Italian
edition which abridged the lengthy original but supplemented it
with numerous quotations from the Fathers.

The *De Gestis* is arranged in the following fifteen Books:[55]

---

[55] The indication of chapters is based on the printed edition at Yale University's
Beinecke Rare Book and Manuscript Library. This copy is entitled *Expositio Super
Totum Corpus Evangeliorum;* the Catalogue identifies it as the first edition from

I. The Mysteries of the Uncreated Word (27 chapters)

II. The Virgin Mary (27 chapters)

III. John the Baptist (3 chapters)

IV. The Life of Christ in General (11 chapters)

V. Christ's Miracles (34 chapters)

VI. The Parables (34 chapters)

VII. The Similitudes (45 chapters)

VIII. The Vices (52 chapters)

IX. The Virtues (54 chapters)

X. The Sermon on the Mount (50 chapters)

XI. Christ's Discourses (55 chapters)

XII. Discourse after the Last Supper (19 chapters)

XIII. The Passion (13 chapters)[56]

XIV. The Resurrection[57]

XV. Christian Justice (46 chapters)

It is apparent from this table of contents that while the *Meditations* was basically chronological in its arrangement the *De Gestis* is topical, thus continuing a pattern which had been long established and which flourished in the succeeding centuries.[58] But this does not mean that chronology was entirely ignored. Books I, II, III, IV, XII, XIII, and XIV form a chronological sequence even though Book III, on John the Baptist, includes some material not from the beginning of the ministry. Furthermore, within the individual Books there is a semblance of chronological arrangement. Thus Book II on the Virgin Mary, and Book XIII on the passion are arranged chronologically. In Book V (Christ's miracles), the chronological approach is explicitly repudiated in favor of a pattern which divides the miracles into two groups according to whether they involve "insensible" or

ca. 1485, printed by Johann Pruess, Strassburg. See the notes on the printed edition in McNeil, *op. cit.,* pp. 60 ff.

[56] The chapters in Book XIII are not numbered, but there are thirteen unnumbered divisions. Actually this is the longest book in the entire volume.

[57] There are no numbered chapters or marked divisions in the edition used.

[58] See, e.g., the many-volumed work of A. Salmeron, *Commentarii in Evangelicam Historiam* (Madrid, 1585 ff.).

"sensible" objects. (This distinction approximates the one made in modern times between nature and healing miracles.) But within these two divisions Fidati followed the approximate sequence of miracles as they are recorded in the Gospels.

The chronological approach cannot be assumed always to be superior to the topical. But in a biography a consideration of chronology is essential, and the writings considered in this chapter have been selected because they represent at least an approach to biographies or "Lives" of Jesus. It is intriguing to note that where the tenets of Rudolf Bultmann are accepted, the chronological "Life" of Jesus is no longer regarded as a possibility and the topical arrangement again emerges as the most appropriate pattern.[59] In the Bultmann tradition the "Life" is topical because it is assumed that a chronology is impossible, while in the fourteenth century the topical form was used because of a lack of interest in the problem of chronology.

Another striking difference between the *Meditations* and *De Gestis* is in the sources utilized. While the author of the former frequently referred to non-biblical sources such as the church fathers of the *Glossa Ordinaria,* Fidati, throughout the entire *De Gestis,* never refers to a single non-biblical source.[60] John of Salerno states that Fidati wrote the entire work without using any book except the Bible, but he also states that Fidati produced the work from memory.[61] Presumably these two statements may be harmonized by assuming that Fidati wrote chiefly from memory and that the only exceptions to this occurred when he checked a biblical passage. The first printed edition is occasionally in error in its citing of the particular Gospel(s) from which material under discussion was borrowed.[62] A comparison of all avail-

---

[59] This is the case with Günther Bornkamm's *Jesus of Nazareth,* trans. Irene and Fraser McLuskey with James M. Robinson (New York: Harper, 1960).

[60] See McNeil, *op. cit.,* p. 175.

[61] *Ibid.,* pp. 72, 39.

[62] For example, Bk. V, chap. 5, refers to Mark in connection with the incident of Matt. 17:24–27 (paying the temple tax) ; Bk. VI, chap. 1, refers to Mark where Matt. 7:7–11 (along with Luke 11:5–13) is apparently intended.

able evidence might clarify whether these errors originated in the printing of that edition or whether they reflect slips of memory on the part of Fidati. The usual procedure in *De Gestis* is for Fidati to begin with an introductory comment, then to quote a passage from the Gospels, and then to follow this with a commentary on the quoted section. It is conceivable that he quoted these passages without reference to the Latin text, but it is more likely that he refreshed his memory from available copies of the Gospels. Fidati's exclusive dependence on the Gospels, as over against the church Fathers, is suggestive of his English contemporary Wycliffe; but there is no evidence that Fidati had any sense of antagonism for the general teaching or policy of the church.[63] There is no good reason to regard him as a pre-Reformation Protestant.

Again, while the *Meditations* avoided the discourses in the Gospels, Fidati gave them special prominence. This is evident from Book X, which devotes fifty chapters to the Sermon on the Mount, and from Book XI, in which fifty-five chapters discuss "Christ's Discourses," chiefly those from the Gospel of John.

It is frequently difficult to determine the attitude of Fidati toward questions of harmonization. His handling of the commentary suggests that he distinguished between the parable of the great supper in Luke 14:15–24 and the similar parable in Matthew 22:1–10;[64] between the healing of the official's son in Matthew 8:5–13 (Luke 7:1–10) and the similar incident in John 4:46–53;[65] and that he ignored some of the Lucan parallels when dealing with the Sermon on the Mount.[66] On the other hand he felt free to equate the parable of the tares in Matthew

---

[63] See McNeil, *op. cit.,* p. 209. While Fidati shared some of the difficulties which confronted the rigorous Fransciscans during this period, there is little evidence of any basic opposition or antagonism to the church in general.

[64] Bk. VI, chaps. 19, 24.

[65] Bk. V, chaps. 12, 18.

[66] Bk. X. The parallels from Luke 6 are generally included along with Matthew's Sermon on the Mount. Some of the parallels in other chapters are included, some omitted.

13:24–30 with that of the seed growing secretly in Mark 4: 26–29;[67] the parable of the talents in Matthew 25:14–30 with that of the pounds in Luke 19:12–27;[68] the various healings of the blind near Jericho in Matthew 20:29–34, Mark 10:46–52, and Luke 18:35–43;[69] and the two versions of the Lord's Prayer in Matthew 6:9–13 and Luke 11:2–4.[70] Since he was more interested in edifying commentary than in chronology he may sometimes have combined incidents for purposes of comment without intending to decide the question of the identity of the incidents thus combined.

The medieval church accepted almost universally the theory of a fourfold meaning in Scripture. This allegorizing tradition was inherited from Hellenism and developed into something like a system by Origen.[71] His threefold pattern, paralleling the distinction between body, soul, and spirit, was later expanded into a fourfold pattern including literal (historical), allegorical (typological), moral (tropological), and anagogical. This fourfold pattern was developed explicitly in John of Cassian's *First Conference with Nesteros*[72] from the early fifth century, but it may have existed as early as Augustine[73] and Jerome.[74] Once established it dominated interpretation until the Reformation. Fidati accepted this technique and refers to it as one of the meanings of John 19:23 ("When the soldiers had crucified Jesus they took his garments and made four parts . . ."),[75] but in fact he seldom developed a fourfold meaning for any one passage. Normally he stressed the moral or tropological meaning, occasionally

[67] Bk. VI, chap. 3.
[68] Bk. VI, chap. 29.
[69] Bk. V, chap. 32.
[70] Bk. X, chaps. 27 ff.
[71] *De Principiis*, Bk. IV, chap. 1, sec. 11 (*The Ante-Nicene Fathers*, Vol. IV).
[72] Chap. 8 (*The Nicene and Post-Nicene Fathers*, Second Series, XI, 437).
[73] *De Genesi ad Litteram* (*Libri duodecim*), Bk. I, chap. 1 (Migne, *Patrologia Latina*, XXXIV, 216–17).
[74] *Commentaria in Ezechielem*, Bk. IV, chap. 16 (Migne, *Patrologia Latina*, XXV, 130).
[75] *De Gestis*, Bk. XIII. See also his discussion of the temple-body "similitude" of John 2:19–21 (Bk. VII, chap. 33).

supplementing this with a second or even third interpretation. Frequently he utilized etymology or numerology in his homilies, but his handling of Greek or Hebrew names does not suggest any significant mastery of these languages.[76]

John of Salerno, as we noted earlier, prepared an Italian edition of Fidati's work for popular consumption. In this edition he condensed sections of the original but amplified the whole by the addition of quotations from the church Fathers. However, the original Latin edition was also popular, as is indicated by the fact that it "was copied not only in Italy, but even more frequently in France, Germany, Switzerland, Austria, Holland, and Belgium."[77] Manifestly the readers were more interested in edification than in historical research. There was genuine interest in the human life of Jesus as an instrument for moral and spiritual instruction, but there was no recognition that the discovery of that human life required explorations beneath the surface of the four Gospels and the accompanying traditions.

IV

While both the *Meditations* and the *De Gestis* were influential during the late Middle Ages and subsequently, their popularity was exceeded by that of the *Vita Christi* by the Carthusian, Ludolphus of Saxony. This conclusion is supported by a comparison of the number of manuscripts, translations, and editions for which there is evidence. Sister Bodenstedt states that there were some sixty editions of the Latin text; to these must be added the partial or complete translations into German, English, Italian, Portuguese, Catalonian, Castilian, and French.[78] While there has been no complete translation into English or German, there have

---

[76] McNeil, *op. cit.*, pp. 103 f.

[77] *Ibid.*, pp. 59 f. See also pp. 211–24 for a partial list of known manuscripts of the *De Gestis*.

[78] Sister Mary Bodenstedt, *The Vita Christi of Ludolphus the Carthusian* (Washington: The Catholic University of America Press, 1944), pp. 19–23.

been a number of French editions including the most recent one by Dom Florent Broquin.[79]

Nothing substantial is known of the youth or early manhood of Ludolphus although the consistent tradition identifying him with Saxony may be accepted as probable. The story that he was a Dominican for many years before becoming a Carthusian does not appear until the sixteenth century but may still be correct.[80] He was prior of the charterhouse at Coblenz from 1343 to 1348. Following his resignation from that office he was at the charterhouse in Mainz and then in Strassburg until his death on April 10, 1377. In addition to his major work, the *Vita Christi,* Ludolphus also published an *Expositio in Psalterium Davidis.* Other minor works are attributed to him, some on the assumption that he was identical with a Dominican Ludolphus, who was also a writer.

The date of the initial appearance of the *Vita Christi* is uncertain, but it is generally held that the bulk of it was prepared during his stay in Mainz, i.e., after 1348. Thus it may have appeared immediately after Fidati's *De Gestis,* and that may explain the absence of any clear dependence on that work. It is appropriate that this work should be called *Vita Christi,* since it is more nearly a true "Life" than either of the two works previously discussed or than any similar work of the preceding centuries.

The *Vita* begins with an explanatory Preface. The main body of the text is divided into two parts, the first having ninety-two chapters and the second, eighty-nine.[81] A significant feature of Ludolphus' division of his work into two parts is that Peter's confession at Caesarea Philippi introduces the second part. It is now generally recognized that in Mark's Gospel this incident

[79] *La Grande Vie de Jesus-Christ* (7 vols.; Paris, 1870–73).

[80] Bodenstedt, *op. cit.,* pp. 1–3.

[81] The edition used in this study is one of several in the Beinecke Rare Book and Manuscript Library at Yale University. It is catalogued as the 1483 edition printed by Anthonius Koburger of Nürnberg. The title is *Meditationes Vitae Jesu Christi.*

represents a turning point in the ministry—although experts do not agree whether this is genuine history or "Marcan" history. At the beginning of Book II Ludolphus states that the passion motif had been missing in the earlier portion of his work but that it will be presented repeatedly from this point on. More than half of the chapters deal with the public ministry of Jesus, i.e., the events between the baptism and the triumphal entry. This indicates that Ludolphus had largely overcome the tendency to concentrate on the birth and the passion.

With respect to the general arrangement of the material it is clear that the author attempted to create a kind of harmony of the Gospels, using as his major guides the two Gospels attributed to actual disciples of Jesus—Matthew and John. However, these guides were not adhered to with absolute rigidity; the events of Matthew 12 are reported in Book I, chapters 71 ff., after the events of Matthew 13–14 have been reported in the immediately preceding chapters. Where John and Matthew differ in the case of the anointing at Bethany, Ludolphus followed the sequence of John (Bk. II, chap. 25). There do not appear to have been any significant shifts in the Johannine order except for the placing of the feeding of the five thousand (John 6) before the events of John 5 (Bk. I, chap. 67). Where Mark or Luke present incidents similar to those in Matthew or John, but in a radically different sequence, Ludolphus was sometimes prepared to equate the incidents and to ignore the sequences of Mark or Luke. Thus he combined the Lucan rejection at Nazareth with the similar narrative in Matthew 13:53–58 (Mark 6:1–6), adopting the relative location required by Matthew's sequence.[82] Again, the events of Mark 1:21–31 (Luke 4:31–39) are placed in Book I, chapter 43, to harmonize with Matthew's location of the healing of Peter's mother-in-law (Matt. 8:14–15). Book I, chapters 33–40 comments on the Sermon on the Mount, including references to a good deal of the Lucan parallel material even when not de-

---

[82] Bk. I, chap. 65.

rived from Luke 6. On the other hand, Ludolphus sometimes prefers to assume a repetition of incidents when differing sequences
occurred in two or more Gospels. Thus the Lucan anointing of
Jesus is reported in Book I, chapter 60, while that of the other
two Synoptics and John appears in Book II, chapter 25; the Johannine call of the first disciples is reported in Book I, chapter 24,
while that of the Synoptists is in Book I, chapter 29, where
Ludolphus separates the Lucan account from that in Matthew
and Mark—thus assuming three "calls."

Occasionally it is difficult to determine what has influenced the
order. For example, Ludolphus places the incident of the Samaritan villagers (Luke 9:51–56) in Book II, chapter 20, even though
putting it there displaces it completely in the Lucan order and
even though Luke is the only evangelist who relates the incident.
Since the immediately preceding chapter had reported the incident of the grateful Samaritan leper (Luke 17:11–19), it is
possible that the occurrence of the Samaritan motif reminded
Ludolphus that he had not yet included the story of the Samaritan
villagers; so he placed it with the other Samaritan incident for
topical rather than chronological reasons. (As is only natural
where Matthew and John are taken as the basic chronological
guides, it is the Lucan order which suffers the most dislocations.)
In the temptation story Ludolphus followed the order of Matthew
but refers to the alternate sequence in Luke, explaining that the
two evangelists differed as to which was the most serious temptation and each therefore placed at the end the one he regarded
as the most serious.[83]

The *Vita* is in no sense merely a retelling of the story found in
the four Gospels. This is obvious from the sheer bulk of the
work, which requires about 2,500 octavo pages. In addition to re-
peating the story Ludolphus engaged in a series of spiritual reflections on the narrative, utilizing the theory of the four senses

[83] Bk. I, chap. 22.

of Scripture[84] and adding the opinions of earlier commentators to enrich his discourse.[85] The literal sense was taken as the basis for the exposition, but frequently there was added a discussion either of the moral (tropological) or the allegorical (typological) sense. Occasionally both of these secondary senses were considered, for example, Book I, chapter 12 (presentation in the temple) and Book I, chapter 13 (flight into Egypt). He utilized the anagogical sense only rarely, for example, Book I, chapter 25 (wedding at Cana) or Book I, chapter 64 (parable of the sower). A good example of a highly developed meditation occurs in Book II, chapter 12, following the story of the rich young ruler. The entire chapter is devoted to the twelve evangelical counsels, beginning with the traditional three, poverty, obedience, and chastity. After these have been discussed Ludolphus lists the twelve precious stones which are symbols of these "counsels." The primarily devotional character of the work is further indicated by the prayers which conclude the Preface and each of the hundred and eighty-one chapters.

Unlike Fidati, but like Pseudo-Bonaventure, Ludolphus used the apocryphal traditions about Jesus with considerable freedom. His Preface contains a defense of this practice and indicates the provisional sense in which these apocryphal traditions are to be accepted.[86] Ludolphus also made extensive use of the rest of the biblical books, quoting from the majority of them.

Sister Bodenstedt compares the *Vita* with the *Meditations* by saying, "In narrative and descriptive power the *Meditations* surpasses the *Vita*. Both works had great influence. The former in-

---

[84] Bk. I, chaps. 25 and 64.

[85] Over eighty earlier authors are referred to by name, the most frequently quoted being Augustine, Chrysostom, Ambrose, Bernard, and Anselm. Of secular writers Cicero and Seneca occur the most frequently. See Bodenstedt, *op. cit.*, pp. 24–52, for a detailed discussion of the sources used by Ludolphus, including a list of the authors named. (The list has been taken from the 1865 Paris edition of Ludolphus.) The *Vita* contains repeated borrowings from the *Meditations* of Pseudo-Bonaventure which we examined earlier.

[86] Bodenstedt, *op. cit.*, p. 47, states that his defense was taken over from the *Meditations*.

spired the literature and art of the late Middle Ages, the latter lives on in the 'Spiritual Exercises.' "[87]

The three writings considered in this chapter appeared in chronological succession. The *Meditations* and the *Vita Christi* stand also in a logical relationship since the *Vita* used the *Meditations* and, from the standpoint here under consideration, represented a development beyond it. The *De Gestis* stands by itself since, so far as can be determined, it did not use the *Meditations* nor was it used by the *Vita Christi.* Of the three works the last, the *Vita Christi,* is the closest approximation to a true "Life" of Christ. From this perspective the *Meditations* is defective in that it slights the public ministry of Christ in order to concentrate on the infancy, the passion, and the resurrection. It is also deficient in that it passes over major blocks of teaching material provided in the Gospels. The *De Gestis* is deficient because of its topical arrangement, which reveals that the author is not seriously concerned with a "Life" in the usual sense of the term.

While there is a line from these writings to the "Lives" of the nineteenth and twentieth centuries this line is not a straight one. It would never have occurred to the fourteenth-century writers that they were engaged in a Quest for the historical Jesus. For them, as for their contemporaries generally, the historical Jesus was plainly portrayed in the pages of the four Gospels. The function of subsequent writers was to transmit this story to their readers in a form that was unified either chronologically or topically. That they produced more than a popularized harmony is traceable to their desire to use the incidents of the readily available material to guide their readers into meditation upon the life of Christ and imitation of that life. Yet even though their "Lives" were not produced out of historical curiosity, these "Lives" are related nonetheless to those of a later date and pattern. By centering their attention on the human life of Jesus for purposes of medi-

[87] *Ibid.,* p. 31.

tation and imitation the three authors considered in this chapter brought the details of that life into the focus of Christian thought and concern. When a newer and more critical historiography emerged, this developed concern led inevitably to a grappling with the question of the historical Jesus. Some of the early church Fathers, such as Augustine, had been aware of the difficulties in the Gospel narratives; this awareness disappeared in the early and late medieval church; it reappeared in the sixteenth century, as we shall see in the next chapter, and became a major driving force in biblical scholarship in the nineteenth century, to which we shall turn our attention in the fifth chapter.

4

Sixteenth-Century
Gospel Harmonies

A striking phenomenon of the study of the Bible in the sixteenth century was the sudden flowering of Gospel harmonies. This movement was the development in the sixteenth century most closely related to the Quest for the historical Jesus. As always, each harmony was an attempt to recover a total picture of the ministry of Jesus with the chronological connections clearly established. Since it was assumed that each Gospel was the work of an evangelist working independently of his predecessors, and that all four were equally valuable historically, the modern phase of the Quest could not yet begin. But within the accepted framework of thought lively differences of opinion emerged, and these differences stimulated discussions which, in the nineteenth century, led to a new approach to the Gospels as sources for the Quest. The nature and extent of the interest in Gospel harmonies during the sixteenth century is impressive witness that a new historical spirit had already begun to emerge in Christendom. In the present survey four aspects or developments in Gospel harmonies during the sixteenth century will be considered:

    I. The sudden increase in the number of harmonies

    II. The emergence of a new format

    III. The "Osiander" pattern in Gospel harmonies

    IV. The "non-Osiander" patterns in Gospel harmonies.

I

The most obvious feature of sixteenth-century Gospel harmonies was their number. There is a dramatic contrast between
the paucity of harmonies in the preceding centuries and their
proliferation in the sixteenth century. It is difficult to determine
the precise number published during that period, but I have
personally investigated, at least in cursory fashion, approximately
thirty different harmonies and am still attempting to locate copies
of an additional half-dozen. Some in this latter group may not be
true harmonies or may be only revisions or translations of harmonies already investigated. On the other hand, there are probably a few titles which I have missed or which have disappeared
entirely. It may be safely estimated that about thirty-five different
Gospel harmonies appeared in the course of the sixteenth century; this number does not include translations from one language
into another nor the various editions in which any one harmony
may have appeared. However, it does include harmonies which
were published in connection with commentaries, e.g., Calvin's
*Commentary on a Harmony of the Evangelists, Matthew, Mark,
and Luke,* or the four-volume *Commentariorum in Evangelicam
Harmoniam* of Thomas Beaux-Amis.[1]

The significance of these statistics is heightened when the
productivity of the sixteenth century is compared with that of the
centuries preceding. It is difficult to know whether the numerous
progeny of Tatian's *Diatessaron* should all be counted as part of
one harmony, but on any rational reckoning it is safe to say that
the sixteenth century produced more harmonies than the combined fourteen centuries that preceded it. Apart from the de-
scendants of Tatian only a handful of harmonies are known from
this entire period. Naturally some allowance must be made for
harmonies which circulated before the age of printing and which
never existed in enough copies to survive the accidents of time.

---

[1] For fuller information on the sixteenth-century harmonies mentioned in the
text, see the Appendix.

Here and there single copies of otherwise unknown harmonies may exist hidden away in libraries, for example, the anonymous thirteenth-century Bible manuscript in the British Museum (Harley MS 2815) which contains the Gospels in the form of a harmony, or an anonymous harmony allegedly prepared at the command of Louis the Pious and once read by Martin Luther.[2] But unless some unknown circumstance induced a peculiarly high mortality rate among harmonies before the sixteenth century, the contrast between the sixteenth and the preceding centuries will remain valid.

As a Protestant I naturally ask whether this plethora of Gospel harmonies was due to the vigorous Protestant interest in the Scriptures; but, unfortunately for this sectarian theory, Roman Catholic harmonies outnumber and precede those by Protestants in the sixteenth century. Furthermore there is little in the prefaces of these harmonies to suggest they were in any sense a product of the distinctively Protestant spirit.

When the harmonists wrote of the reasons for their work they usually mentioned one or both of the following two reasons: to edify the faithful by the presentation of a total picture of Christ's life and ministry; or, to refute the critics of the Gospels by demonstrating the essential and astonishing agreement of the Gospels. This is clear enough. But since edification and apologetic were perennial interests of the church, these explanations leave unanswered the further question, namely, why did edification and apologetic take precisely this turn in the sixteenth century? Probably the answer to this is that in the centuries immediately before the sixteenth an increasing historical interest emerged alongside of long-established theological and devotional concerns. This new interest made itself felt also within the church; hence it was believed that presentations of a total picture of the career of Jesus would be helpful for edification. At the same

---

[2] See the reference in J. A. Fabricius, *Bibliotheca Graeca* (rev. ed. by G. C. Harles; Hamburg, 1790–1812), IV, 882.

time, outside the church historical questions were raised about the
Gospels which had not been raised since the days of Celsus,
Porphyry, or Julian the Apostate. The church defended its Scriptures by appealing to the remarkable degree of unity between
the four Gospels—an agreement which is indeed dramatic so
long as one assumes that each of the four originated in total in-
dependence of the others. This assumption was universal throughout the sixteenth century. Gospel harmonies and the discussions
accompanying them were a defense against the critics and a comfort
to believers. A seventeenth-century harmonist spoke of his work
as a means of strengthening the faithful against "Jews and
Turks."[3]

A purely external reason for part of the increase in the number of Gospel harmonies may have been the development of
movable type in the fifteenth century. Estimates vary as to the
actual increase in the production of books occasioned by these
technological developments, but it is certain that there was a substantial increase in the number of new titles appearing each year.
However, even the most exaggerated estimate of the impact of
printing would be inadequate to explain the sudden multiplication of harmonies in the sixteenth century. Basically this phenomenon must be explained by the new interests and new questions which had arisen concerning history, biblical or secular.

II

A second feature of sixteenth-century Gospel harmonies was the
emergence of a new format, namely, that of the harmony arranged
in parallel columns. Some use the term "synopsis" for this new
format, reserving the name "harmony" for the work in which
the different Gospel narratives are woven together into a single,
consecutive narrative (as in Tatian's *Diatessaron,* for example).
This distinction is not consistently followed in English, and it

[3] See the Preface to Johannes Christianus, *Harmonia Evangelistarum* (1642).

will be simpler to distinguish the two types by using "harmony" in a broad sense and then speaking of the "integrated harmony" as over against the "parallel harmony."

Who authored the first parallel harmony? A definite answer is not easy to give, for reasons that will become obvious. The Protestant Charles Du Moulin (Carolus Molinaeus) certainly used such an arrangement in his *Collatio et Unio Quatuor Evangelistarum Domini Nostri Jesu Christi* (1565). Probably this new format was also used in the harmony by Paul Crell published in 1566. I have seen only the German edition of 1571, and it is arranged as a parallel harmony. In the Preface Crell comments that many previous harmonies had been attempted but that since they wove the four Gospels into a single narrative they inevitably omitted some phrases or even entire versions of some stories. Crell explains that to obviate this shortcoming he has arranged his materials in parallel columns so that each Gospel may be studied in its own right. It is of particular interest that Crell's harmony was, by his own statement, a continuation of the work begun by his mentor Johann Bugenhagen, who was active in Wittenberg and elsewhere in the early days of the Reformation. It is uncertain whether the parallel columns were Crell's own idea or whether they had been used by Bugenhagen in his preliminary drafts. The new format also appeared in the *Chronologia* (1569) of Gerhard Mercator, the cosmographer, who may be classified either as Protestant or Catholic depending on one's taste. In this work Mercator included a partial harmony arranged in parallel columns. It was a "partial harmony," because, in order to abbreviate, Mercator frequently included only the opening and closing sections of pericopes. In 1592, in the closing months of his life, Mercator published a complete harmony following the same pattern which had appeared in his *Chronologia* of 1569.

The new format was not a distinctively Protestant interest. It appeared also in the *Syntaxis Historiae Evangelicae* (1572) of Alan Cope, a Roman Catholic, as well as in the *Commentariorum in Evangelicam Harmoniam* of the Carmelite Thomas Beaux-Amis which began to appear in 1583.

These are the earliest examples of complete harmonies in the parallel format with which I am familiar. However, when John Calvin published his commentaries on the Gospels he arranged the Synoptic Gospels in the form of a harmony. This commentary, which first appeared in 1555, presented the Synoptic material in parallel columns, though of course it did not include the Gospel of John, which was dealt with in separate volumes. Again, the harmony of Andreas Osiander (first edition, 1537) was an integrated harmony, but the author attached to it an *Elenchus* or Summary which presented the Gospel materials in condensed form but arranged in four vertical columns. While this was a condensation it ran to some twenty-two large pages and gave a complete picture of Osiander's views concerning the relationship between incidents in the various Gospels. In one sense this was the first of the parallel harmonies.

But even this is not the whole story. Thus far I have included as parallel harmonies only those in which vertical parallel columns were used. Yet it is apparent that the same general purposes could be served through the use of horizontal columns, or, more precisely, through a harmony in which the various versions of a single incident were reported *ad seriatim.* Such an arrangement would not be as convenient as our present parallel harmonies with vertical columns, but in principle it accomplished the same result, i.e., the preservation of the integrity of each Gospel, plus the presentation of the materials from all four Gospels so that a comparison could be made. A harmony with horizontal parallel columns was prepared before any of the parallel harmonies just mentioned. It was published in 1535 by Robert Goullet, a Roman Catholic professor of sacred theology in Paris, with the title *Tetramonon Evangeliorum.* It was divided into one hundred seventy-six "rubrics," many of which had still further subdivisions. His Rubric 50 presented the various versions of the feeding of the

five thousand. First came the Matthean account with the nota-
tion Matthew 14 B,C; then came Mark 6 D,E,F; then Luke 9 B;
and, finally, John 6 A,B. Parenthetically, the first occurrence of
verse divisions in a harmony was probably in John Calvin's *Commentary on a Harmony of the Evangelists,* which was produced
by the printer-editor Robert Stephanus, who had introduced these
divisions in 1551. They soon become common in both Protestant
and Roman Catholic harmonies as well as in Bibles generally.
Prior to that time the thirteenth-century chapter divisions had
been used, sometimes with the addition of lettered subdivisions,
as in the Goullet harmony just mentioned.

   Lest it be assumed that all wisdom in the matter of format
originated in the sixteenth century, it should be observed that
even Goullet was not the first to prepare a parallel harmony with
horizontal columns. The same pattern had been followed by
Guido de Perpignan about 1300 in his *Quattuor Unum—Hoc
Est Concordia Evangelica.* While Goullet did not refer explicitly
to his predecessor it is likely that he was familiar with his work
and may have borrowed the principle from him.

   It may seem that an undue amount of space has been used on
a purely external question, the question of format. Yet a little
consideration will indicate that this development in external form
reflected a corresponding shift in the interests of the harmonists.
The integrated harmony met the needs of those who were concerned solely for a unified portrait of the total ministry of Jesus.
The individual who created such a harmony was compelled to
wrestle with the problems of harmonization, but the readers
were freed from this problem since the work had been done for
them and the traces of those labors vanished in the finished
product. But the moment it became important to the harmonists
that their readers should understand the problems of harmonization, and how a particular harmony met those problems, at that
moment it became necessary for a new format to replace the old.
The parallel harmony allowed the reader to evaluate the prob-

lems of order and the proposals of the harmonists with respect
to those problems. Since the sixteenth century only one major advance has been made in the format of Gospel harmonies, namely,
the recognition that each Gospel should be retained in its own
order but that incidents in any Gospel should be repeated when
a parallel incident in another Gospel occurs in a different order.
This leads to the repetition of many incidents, but it is the only
objective method for giving the reader the necessary information
on any particular passage. While this principle is recognized in
many modern harmonies it is practically never carried out with
complete consistency, presumably because of the concern for
space and expense.

That the new format was the result of new interests and not
merely an accidental development is confirmed by the fact that
even in the old-style integrated harmonies devices emerged to
express the new interests. Thus the main body of Andreas Osiander's harmony was integrated, but he introduced into this material a series of letters to indicate the relationship of the various
phrases to the individual Gospels. He exhausted nearly the entire alphabet to show which Gospel or combination of Gospels
was represented by a single phrase or word. There were letters
for each individual Gospel, letters for the possible combinations
of two, three, or four Gospels, and letters for the relevant phrases
which he included from Acts or I Corinthians 15. An interesting
feature of this rather complicated system of lettering was that it
reappeared in subsequent harmonies, Roman Catholic as well as
Protestant. Thus Cornelius Jansen, a Roman Catholic, reproduced
the Osiander lettering system in his widely used *Concordia
Evangelica,* a work which first appeared in the year 1549. In at
least some editions even Jansen's explanatory chart of symbols corresponds in arrangement with that used by Osiander—an early and
commendable illustration of ecumenical cooperation in academic
matters! Even before Osiander, Michael Memler in his integrated
harmony of 1524—which was really only a repetition of Victor of

Capua's translation of Tatian—utilized the Eusebian Sections and Canons to indicate the differing contributions of the individual Gospels.

Thus, in the sixteenth century, both the number of harmonies and the experimentation in format support the thesis that a new interest in historical questions and answers had arisen. No precise date can be given for the emergence of this interest, but certainly it appeared well before the sixteenth century. It may be significant that the previously mentioned anonymous harmony in the British Museum,[4] from the thirteenth century, presents an integrated text, but the Gospels from which a particular section are drawn are indicated in colored letters at the beginning of the section. Concerns which had been dormant for centuries were stirring again. They would not reach their maximum intensity until the nineteenth and twentieth centuries, however, when New Testament scholarship became preoccupied with an almost frenzied Quest for the historical Jesus.

III

A third feature of sixteenth-century Gospel harmonies, especially among Protestants, was the prevalence of what may be identified as the "Osiander" pattern. This pattern, which appeared in Osiander's harmony of 1537, rested on two principles: one, each Gospel should be presented in its own sequence, and, two, if there are significant differences of detail between two versions of an incident they should be regarded as separate incidents even though they occur at the same chronological points in the narrative. These principles are illustrated in his handling of the healing of the blind near Jericho. Luke's version presents this incident before the entry into Jericho and the meeting with Zacchaeus, while Matthew and Mark agree in placing the incident following the departure from Jericho. (The reference to Jericho in both Matthew and Mark is curiously unmotivated.) Following

---

[4] See p. 87 above.

principle one Osiander therefore distinguishes the Lucan healing
from that in Matthew or Mark. However, while Matthew and
Mark agree in their chronological arrangement they differ in that
Mark speaks of one blind man while Matthew mentions two.
Here, following principle two, Osiander distinguishes the Matthean from the Marcan incident. The result? Osiander reports a
total of three separate healing incidents in the vicinity of Jericho
involving all together, four blind men.

Anyone familiar with the Gospels, particularly with the Synoptics, will be aware of the innumerable complications inevitably
created by these principles of Osiander. In addition to the tripling
of the healings near Jericho the following triplications also occur:

the centurion's servant (son): John 4:46–53, Matthew 8:5–13,
and Luke 7:1–10

anointings of Jesus: Luke 7:36–50, John 12:1–8, and Matthew
26:6–13 (Mark 14:3–9)

cleansing of the temple: John 2:13–17, Matthew 21:12–13 (Luke
19:45–46), and Mark 11:15–19

Following the same principles Osiander created a considerable
number of "doublets" where a less doctrinaire approach would
have found only a single incident. Here are some illustrations:

healing of a leper: Matthew 8:1–4 and Mark 1:40–45 (Luke 5:
12–16)

the Gadarene demoniac(s): Matthew 8:28–34 and Mark 5:1–20
(Luke 8:26–39)

Jairus' daughter and the woman with a hemorrhage: Matthew
9:18–26 and Mark 5:21–43 (Luke 8:40–56)

Beelzebub controversy: Matthew 12:24 ff. and Mark 3:22 ff.
(Luke 11:14 ff.)

the question of David's son: Matthew 22:41–46 and Mark 12:
35–37 (Luke 20:41–44)

betrayal by Judas predicted: Matthew 26:20–25 (Mark 14:17–
21) and Luke 22:21–23

Peter's denial predicted: Matthew 26:33–35 (Mark 14:29–31) and Luke 22:31–34

Furthermore, Osiander presented the Sermon on the Mount (Matthew 5–7) without any parallels whatsoever; the same was true in his handling of the Sermon on the Plain (Luke 6:20–49). For the entire travel narrative of Luke 9:51–18:14 his arrangement allowed only a single parallel, i.e., Mark 10:10–12, which was regarded as a parallel to Luke 16:18 (the divorce logion). It is somewhat ironic that, contrary to most modern scholars, he allowed only this one small parallel to Luke's travel narrative— but this one parallel is not regarded as a parallel by modern scholars!

Yet even Osiander suffered from a "failure of nerve" when it came to a consistent application of his principles. Thus he transferred Matthew 12:1–14 (plucking grain on the Sabbath, healing a withered hand) from its original location and placed it after Matthew 9:34; and he recorded only three temptations of Jesus although the differences between Matthean and Lucan order would have justified a repetition of one of the temptations. For this inconsistency he was rebuked by a successor, Charles du Moulin, who in his *Collatio et Unio Quatuor Evangelistarum Domini Nostri Jesu Christi* replaced Matthew 12:1–14 in its own order as he endeavored to carry out Osiander's principles with even greater rigidity. Incidentally, Moulin was sharply critical of Calvin, whose attitude in such matters was almost the opposite of that represented by Osiander. Few others were as rigid in the application of these principles as Osiander and Moulin, but their general pattern left clear marks on the work of Matthias Flacius Illyricus, Gerhard Mercator, Laurentius Codomann, Martin Chemnitz, and Bartholomew Scultetus. The harmony of the last named was notable in that Scultetus felt himself competent to identify, in most instances, the year, month, and day in which the particular incidents occurred.

Thus the majority of Protestant harmonies in the sixteenth

century followed the Osiander pattern. On the other hand, no Roman Catholic approached the extremes of Osiander or Moulin —unless Mercator is counted as a Catholic. Some Roman Catholic harmonists appear to have made considerable use of Osiander's second principle, namely, that differences in detail mean that separate incidents are being presented and not separate versions of the same incident. This is true of Cornelius Jansen, who, as already noted, borrowed Osiander's lettering system.[5] It is also true, in some measure, of Jean du Buisson's *Historia et Harmonia Evangelica* (1571). It is difficult to determine why the Roman Catholic harmonists consistently rejected Osiander's other principle and made no serious attempt to preserve the integrity of the sequence in all four Gospels. Was it because of the sound historical insight that the evangelists had no great concern with chronology? Or was it due to the harmonists' own lack of concern for chronological arrangement? Or was it due to the influence of Augustine, who had asserted explicitly and repeatedly that the Gospel writers sometimes followed the order of recollection rather than that of the events themselves? The last explanation is the most likely both because of the authority generally assigned to Augustine and because of the specific references to his *Harmony of the Gospels*.[6]

If it is assumed that it is the Protestant rigidity that requires explanation rather than the Roman flexibility, then an answer is perfectly obvious. In their struggle against the total authority of the Roman church the Protestants were formulating a concept of the total authority of Scripture. The simplest version of such a concept would include the affirmation of an inerrancy reaching to all details of fact as well as of doctrine. The Osiander pattern

---

[5] See p. 92 above.

[6] A later Roman Catholic harmonist, Caesar Becillus Urbinatus, obviously building on Augustine, was able to state in his *Evangeliorum Connexio* (1623) precisely how often each Gospel departed from the exact chronological sequence and how many of these departures were "by anticipation" and how many were "by recapitulation." (On these Augustinian phrases see above, chapter 2.)

was the natural outgrowth of such an emphasis, though it is highly significant that neither Luther nor Calvin understood the Gospel narratives as did Osiander. Both Luther and Calvin were certain that the evangelists had not always followed the order of history in their presentations.[7]

IV

The final section of this chapter is concerned with the non-Osiander patterns in sixteenth-century Gospel harmonies. Unfortunately these patterns cannot be neatly summarized. In some harmonists the reader suspects that the basic pattern was a lack of pattern, i.e., the harmonist made adjustments at this point or that without any clearcut principle of harmonization. However, it may be helpful to deal with two or three individual harmonies and then to indicate directions which prevailed in several.

Having dealt at length with Osiander, whose dubious influence dominated the Protestant scene, it may be well to turn now to John Calvin who, while unquestionably a Protestant, stood at an extreme distance from the Osiander position on harmonization. It has long been noted that there appears to be tension between Calvin's abstract statements concerning the doctrine of Scripture and the assumptions implicit in his historical-exegetical work. His theory was rigid, his practice was flexible—or at least so it seems. From the theological statements in the *Institutes of the Christian Religion* one would expect Calvin to have agreed with the principles of Osiander, but his *Commentary on a Harmony of the Evangelists* refutes this expectation. In this work he explicitly repudi-

[7] In his *Commentary on a Harmony of the Evangelists, Matthew, Mark, and Luke,* trans. William Pringle (3 vols.; Edinburgh, 1845–46; reprinted, Eerdmans, 1956), Calvin refers scornfully to Osiander; see his comments on Matt. 20:29 ff. (and parallels) or on Luke 22:24 ff. The references and quotations from Calvin in the following paragraphs are all from the *Commentary* and will be found there under the passage or parable cited in the text.

For Luther's attitude see, e.g., his discussion of John 2:13 f. in Jaroslav Pelikan (ed.), *Sermons on the Gospel of John, Chapters 1–4 (Luther's Works,* Vol. XXII [St. Louis: Concordia Publishing House, 1957], pp. 218 f.).

ated the Osiander approach and affirmed his dependence on attitudes toward harmonization which had appeared in Martin Bucer's Gospel commentaries. Unlike Osiander, but like Augustine and Bucer, Calvin did not assume that the sequence in the individual Gospels was necessarily intended to be historical. In connection with comments on Matthew 4:18 he wrote:

> . . . for no fixed and distinct order of dates was observed by the Evangelists in composing their narratives. The consequence is that they disregard the order of time, and satisfy themselves with presenting in a summary manner, the leading transactions in the life of Christ. They attended, no doubt, to the years, so as to make it plain to their readers, in what manner Christ was employed, during the course of three years, from the commencement of his preaching till his death. But miracles, which took place about the same time are freely intermixed; which will afterwards appear more clearly from many examples. . . .

Repeated statements of this type reflect Calvin's indifference to one of Osiander's basic assumptions, i.e., the integrity of the chronological sequence in the separate Gospels.

But Calvin was equally free when it came to identifying incidents reported in two or more Gospels, even though there were some differences in the details of these incidents. Thus he had only one call of the four fisherman, one healing of the Gadarene demoniac(s), and one healing of the blind near Jericho. He equated Matthew's parable of the marriage feast (Matt. 22:1–14) and parable of the talents (Matt. 25:14–30) with the similar parables in Luke 14:15–24 and Luke 19:12–27 respectively. He commented on the quite explicit chronological difference concerning the day of the cleansing of the temple as reported in Mark on the one hand and Matthew and Luke on the other. He then made his own suggestions, but added, "But anyone who will consider how little care the Evangelists bestowed on pointing out dates will not stumble at this diversity in the narrative."

Probably Calvin's first principle was to equate sections in one

Gospel with those in another whenever possible. Thus he presented a whole series of parallels with Matthew 5–7—practically all those from Luke or Mark which would appear in any modern harmony. But while this principle tends to reduce the total number of incidents to be arranged, it does not suggest in what order they should be presented. It is difficult to determine what principle Calvin used at this point. It is clear that in the Synoptics it was Matthew which suffered the fewest rearrangements, although there is no evidence that this was a conscious principle on Calvin's part. It is likely that he made his decisions from section to section but that the clarity of Matthew's outline and the traditional view of its priority resulted in a relative preference for its sequence.

Few Roman Catholics went as far as Calvin in identifying incidents in one Gospel with similar incidents reported in other Gospels, though Robert Goullet (1535) and Joachim Perion (1553) were nearly as free. In view of their dates it is obvious that they could not have been dependent on Calvin but represented a similar mood in Roman Catholic thought.

While Robert Goullet was comparatively free in his equation of incidents despite differences of detail, it is difficult to discover an overall pattern in his arrangement. Study of his outline makes it clear that he, like many harmonists of this period, preserved the Johannine sequence practically without change. But what was the principle he used with respect to the bulk of the Synoptic material? I was unable to answer this question until, noting his admiring references to the *Concordia Evangelica* produced about 1400 by John Gerson, I compared his *Tetramonon Evangeliorum* with this earlier work. It was then apparent that Gerson had been his basic guide. Like Gerson he divided his work into three parts, although he had one hundred seventy-six subdivisions in place of Gerson's one hundred fifty. In general he followed the order of Gerson, but while Gerson gave primacy to the orders of John and Matthew, Goullet's departures from this principle in his *Tetramonon* obscured the definitive role of Matthew. It is unlikely that

Goullet consciously subordinated Matthew. It is more probable that he followed Gerson's order, making occasional *ad hoc* adjustments, and these improvisations happened to obscure the role Gerson originally intended for Matthew.

Reference was just made to the preservation of the Johannine order as a principle of harmony arrangement. It appeared not only in the previously mentioned work of Robert Goullet but also in the harmonies of Cornelius Jansen (1549), Alan Cope (1572), and Thomas Beaux-Amis (1583 ff.), to mention the most obvious examples. The primacy given to John may have been due either to principle or to expediency. Once it was generally accepted that the ministry of Jesus had included three (or four) Passovers the simplest procedure was to accept John as providing the overall pattern and then to work the Synoptic material into the framework thus provided. However, it is probable that principle also played a role, since the author of the Fourth Gospel was everywhere regarded as "the beloved disciple" and tradition taught that he had prepared his work to correct and supplement that of the three Synoptic evangelists.

If John's sequence was most frequently preserved without significant rearrangement, Matthew's occupied the second most favored position. Except for the Osiander-type harmonies Matthew's order was probably never followed without some adjustment, particularly in the early chapters, but generally its sequence was less disturbed than that of Mark or Luke.[8] Again, it is difficult to know to what extent the special place accorded Matthew was a matter of principle as over against convenience. But it is certainly no accident that the two Gospels whose sequences were most strictly observed were the two Gospels assigned by ancient tradition to "apostles," while the other two evangelists were only "apostolic men," i.e., associates of apostles.

An unusual exception to the stress on John and Matthew ap-

---

[8] See, e.g., the harmonies of Antonius Broickius of Königstein (1539) or Jean du Buisson (1571).

pears in the harmony of Paul Crell which appeared in 1566. I have seen only the 1571 German edition but in this latter edition it is explicitly stated by the author that he has given preference to the order of John and Mark. Thus Crell was possibly an early forerunner of the nineteenth-century preference for Mark.

While developments in the sixteenth century indicate a lively interest in the relationship of the four Gospels to one another, no real progress in this direction was possible until it became clear that some form of written interdependence existed between the Synoptics. This realization did not come until the nineteenth century, the period which saw the blossoming of the modern Quest for the historical Jesus.

5

The Modern Phase
of the
Quest

This chapter will attempt to summarize nearly two hundred years of New Testament scholarship in an effort to indicate how the modern phase of the Quest for the historical Jesus has brought us to the point where we now are. According to the conventional view Reimarus was the father of this new development, and I shall accept this conventional view despite the legitimate questions which may be raised concerning his paternity.

I

Hermann Samuel Reimarus was born in amburg, Germany, in 1694. He studied theology, classical philology, and philosophy, spent a year or two traveling in Holland and England, and then, as a comparatively young man, became professor of Hebrew and Oriental languages at the *Gymnasium* in Hamburg. He continued at this post for more than forty years, until his death in 1768. During these years his academic duties were light, and he was able to develop his own interests. He published a distinguished edition of Dio Cassius, thus completing the work begun by his father-in-law, J. A. Fabricius. He also wrote books on natural religion, a subject much in vogue during the eighteenth century. A different facet of his interests was reflected in his publication of a book on the instincts of animals. All this work was competently done, but Reimarus created no great excitement in his own generation, though Schweitzer was guilty of pardonable exaggeration when he said, "For his contemporaries he had no existence. . . ."[1]

It was a posthumous publication that secured his niche in history. During his life his secret enthusiasm had been a manuscript which he revised repeatedly and showed to only a few intimates. In its final form it ran to some four thousand handwritten pages and was called "An Apology or Defense of the Rational Worship of God." Two copies of this manuscript exist, one in the library of Göttingen University and the other in the State and Municipal Library of Hamburg. The document has never been published in its entirety, although when I inquired for the manuscript at the Hamburg library in the summer of 1962 I was told that tentative approval had been given for its publication. After Reimarus' death a copy of the manuscript, but not the final revision, passed somewhat mysteriously into the hands of the philosopher G. E. Lessing. He attempted to publish the entire work but the government censor refused permission. Not to be defeated, Lessing then published a number of excerpts in a journal for which he was responsible and over which the censor had no jurisdiction. In order to protect Reimarus' reputation Lessing published the so-called "Fragments" anonymously, but with a rather broad hint that they were from the pen of a certain J. L. Schmidt who had been safely dead for a number of years and who had an already well-established reputation as a heretic. Four of the seven Fragments dealt with the biblical narrative. The most famous of these, by all odds the longest and the one which most concerns us here, was called "The Aims of Jesus and His Disciples."[2] It might have been en-

[1] Albert Schweitzer, *The Quest of the Historical Jesus,* trans. W. Montgomery (1st Eng. ed.; London: Black, 1910), p. 14.

[2] It was published separately, as a book, in Braunschweig in 1778, under the title, *Vom dem Zwecke Jesu und seiner Jünger.* Lessing was given as the editor but Reimarus' name was still not revealed, the authorship being concealed in the subtitle, *Noch ein Fragment des Wolfenbüttelschen Ungenannten.* An English

titled, "The Aims of Jesus as Distinguished from Those of His Disciples."

Before commenting on this work it should be noted that some of Reimarus' ideas were not original. He had been in contact with English deists during his brief stay in that country, he continued to read their works during his career in Hamburg, and in his manuscript he referred explicitly to two of them, John Tolland and Anthony Collins—though his references to them were in connection with Old rather than New Testament problems. In 1744, some years before Lessing's publication of the Fragments, Peter Annet, an English deist, published a treatise entitled *The Resurrection of Jesus Christ Reconsidered,* which paralleled the thought of Reimarus concerning the discontinuity between the teaching of Jesus and that of his disciples in the following generation. But it is likely that Reimarus' views on this point were formulated before 1744. Fortunately, the question of who influenced whom is not essential for our present purpose.

At the outset of his study (Part I, section 3) Reimarus laid down the principle that while Jesus is presented both in the Gospels and in the Epistles it is solely from the former that the historical Jesus can be discovered. He insisted on this contrast between the Gospels and the Epistles with the greatest emphasis, but the reader does not fully understand this insistence until he has read the second half of "The Aims of Jesus and His Disciples." There he discovers that, according to Reimarus, the disciples were totally disillusioned when nothing happened after the death of Jesus. Then, rather than abandon the interesting and profitable life they had become accustomed to as wandering preachers with Jesus, they fabricated the resurrection stories and transformed the

translation of the second half of Reimarus' book, by an anonymous translator but bearing the name of Charles Voysey as editor, was published in 1879 under the title *Fragments from Reimarus, Consisting of Brief Critical Remarks on the Object of Jesus and His Disciples as Seen in the New Testament* (London and Edinburgh: Williams and Norgate; now reprinted, Lexington, Ky.: American Theological Seminary Library Association, 1962).

message of Jesus into a new religion complete with a set of doctrines of which Jesus had known nothing. A more unlikely explanation of the contrast between the teaching of Jesus and that of the primitive church is difficult to imagine! The modern reader discovers in Reimarus a curious combination of shrewd observations, which are helpful even today, and fantastic theories which could not survive the greater historical insight of the nineteenth century. It has been observed that the eighteenth century was the century of ideas and the nineteenth, the century of facts, or perhaps of history understood as facts. Reimarus, like ourselves, was a child of his own age; but our amusement at his follies, rather than strengthening our conceit, should serve to remind us that subsequent generations will laugh at our follies—unless, of course, these follies eliminate mankind entirely from the earthly scene.

Having proclaimed a basic contrast between the Jesus of the Gospels and the Jesus of the Epistles, Reimarus turned to the investigation of the Gospels. He assured his readers that all four are in substantial agreement and that, therefore, they cannot have been guilty of extensive distortion or omission. According to Reimarus the center of Jesus' message was the proclamation of the kingdom of God—a kingdom understood, however, in the traditional Jewish sense, i.e., as a visible, political kingdom. In this kingdom Jesus expected to reign as Messiah. In the light of this expectation he called men to repentance and to belief (a) in his message; (b) in his wonder-working power, and; (c) in his coming Messiahship. But he did not challenge the established ceremonial system and introduced no non-Jewish theological ideas. When nothing happened after his death the disciples finally emerged from their disillusionment and then, with cunning and deliberate deception, announced a resurrection. They transferred the expectation of a kingdom from the immediate present to a more distant, future second coming and universalized the message so it could be proclaimed to Gentiles as well as Jews. It was the disciples, too, who eliminated the old Jewish ceremonials which hampered wide-scale missionary activity. It was also they who transformed certain Jewish customs into Christian sacraments and who created a new theological system with Trinity, atonement through the death of Jesus, spiritual regeneration, and the other characteristic motifs of the Epistles and later Christian teaching. On the basis of this drastic revision the original movement had a rebirth and spread throughout the Roman Empire.

In this chapter I must confine myself to a description of the development without engaging in a critique of the particular stages of that development. But I cannot refrain from pointing out the most obvious absurdity in the reconstruction of the beginnings of Christianity as imagined by Reimarus. If the apostles deliberately and consciously transformed the message of Jesus into something totally other than that which it had been originally, how does it happen that the same group of apostles, and those associated with them, perpetuated an untransformed version of the ministry of Jesus, that is to say, the version which has come down to us in the Gospels? It is easy to assert that the Epistles reflect a transformed version of Jesus' teaching while the Gospels reflect the original tradition. But if the transformation was the result of a conscious and planned deception why did those same deceivers refute themselves by perpetuating the untransformed tradition alongside of the transformed?

This objection cannot be overcome without a serious modification of some element in the hypothesis of Reimarus. One could assume perhaps that the apostles did not transform the original teaching, but in that case Reimarus would have to begin his work all over again since such an assumption ruins his whole hypothesis. Or one could argue that the apostles did transform the tradition but were unaware that they had done so; therefore they perpetuated also the original tradition without being aware of the clash— and the two traditions lived in peace, side by side, until the days of Reimarus! Or, thirdly, one could argue that the apostles transformed the entire tradition and that it is this transformed tradition which we meet both in the Epistles and in the Gospels. Those who are familiar with Gospel studies in our generation will recognize that it is this last alternative which is currently most widely discussed.

II

However, we cannot jump directly from Reimarus to the present. What happened during the intervening generations? For those who desire a more encyclopedic presentation Albert Schweitzer's book, *The Quest of the Historical Jesus,* remains the basic text, although additional materials must be used for the developments of the past half-century. For the present purpose an adequate picture may be obtained by following one strand of the development down to our own century. When the twentieth century is reached, the picture inevitably becomes more complicated since we do not yet have sufficient perspective to distinguish main lines from those which are only secondary. The one strand I wish to pursue is that of the attitude toward the sources. This is the key to the development during the nineteenth century and also, to a degree, the key to the complexity of the problems which confront us today. The development of the attitude toward the sources has not been a single, steady, consistent development. But for the purposes of clarity the logical development of the thought may be followed without regard for the precise chronological pattern. I will not burden the reader with a multiplicity of names as I attempt to sketch five stages in this development.

The *first stage* had begun even before Reimarus when some writers, chiefly early English deists, contrasted the religion of the New Testament with that which emerged in the creeds of the early Christian centuries. So far as our task is concerned they were saying that the Jesus of history should be reconstructed from the pages of the New Testament without regard for the theological formulations of the later church, notably at Nicea (A.D. 325) and

Chalcedon (A.D. 451). Parenthetically it may be noted that the fourth and fifth centuries were concerned with the Quest of the theological Christ in a way that parallels the Quest for the historical Jesus in the eighteenth to the twentieth centuries. It would be hazardous to predict whether the completed work of the most recent centuries will last as long as has that of the fourth and fifth centuries.

While at this first stage the entire New Testament was regarded as the basic source for discovering the historical Jesus, the *second stage* began when the four Gospels were set apart as the sole legitimate sources for the Quest. This, it will be remembered, was the position taken by Reimarus, though it is entirely likely that he had borrowed it from the English deists. I mention the English deists again since in some quarters it is customary to speak as if all the perversity associated with New Testament criticism had its origin in German scholarship. It is salutary to remember that the beginnings of this movement were in English deism, though it remains true that nineteenth-century German scholars carried on New Testament research with such indefatigable vigor that German names are those most frequently associated with these developments.

Reimarus has been mentioned as a representative of this second stage, in which the sources for the life of Jesus had been reduced to the four Gospels. In the published version of "The Aims of Jesus and His Disciples" he used only the four Gospels as authoritative and he used them all as equally authoritative, though he questioned the authenticity of the baptismal formula in Matthew 28:18–20. But it is reported[3] that in the final version of his manuscript Reimarus indicated a change in his thinking and was inclined to use the Fourth Gospel only with reserve. In any event this constituted the *third stage* in the development of the attitude toward the sources for the life and teaching of Jesus:

[3] See D. F. Strauss, *Hermann Samuel Reimarus* (Leipzig: Brockhaus, 1862), pp. 203 ff.

the three Synoptic Gospels were made the basis for this research. The literary, theological, and historical differences between John and the Synoptics had long been noted. Clement of Alexandria, writing about A.D. 200, said: "John, perceiving that the external facts [*ta sōmatika*] had been set forth in the Gospels [i.e., in the Synoptics], was urged on by his disciples, and, divinely moved by the Spirit, composed a spiritual Gospel [*pneumatikon . . . euangelion*]."[4] Many other scholars of the early church, and later, recognized the contrast of style and content between the Synoptics and John. However, none of these scholars concluded that the Johannine material was therefore historically inferior to that in the Synoptics. In fact, as was pointed out in chapter 4, John's Gospel frequently provided the historical framework within which the information supplied by the other Gospels was set. But now John was set aside as a basic source in the Quest for the historical Jesus, and the number of primary sources was reduced to three, the Synoptic Gospels. This did not happen overnight. The serious questions that had been raised about John before the end of the eighteenth century did not achieve significant influence. In the early nineteenth century Schleiermacher used John along with the Synoptics in writing his life of Jesus; in fact his favorite texts concerning the "God-consciousness" of Jesus were taken from John. But when in June, 1835, David Friederich Strauss published the first edition of his *Life of Jesus,* his rejection of the historicity of John's Gospel became the center of prolonged discussion. Although Strauss was bitterly attacked, and although the substantial historicity of John has been defended by able scholars, the trend of the times for the past hundred years has been to use John's Gospel sparingly and with great caution in any reconstruction of the life of Jesus.[5]

[4] Quoted in Eusebius, *Ecclesiastical History,* Bk. VI, chap. 14, sec. 7. (The translation in the text is my own.)

[5] The present generation has seen a revival of interest in the historical tradition underlying the Fourth Gospel. See most recently C. H. Dodd, *Historical Tradition in the Fourth Gospel* (Cambridge University Press, 1963).

The *fourth stage* in the handling of the sources arrived with the emergence of the two-source theory for the Synoptic Gospels. For centuries the church had read the Gospels assuming, except perhaps for Augustine, that they were totally independent witnesses to the narratives related. But now an enormous amount of intensive work was done on the peculiar relationship between large sections of the Synoptic Gospels. Could the striking verbal similarities, not only in direct speech but also in narrative, be explained by the role of the Holy Spirit in the production of these Gospels? But if the Holy Spirit was the source of striking similarities of phraseology, how were the dissimilarities to be explained, particularly when some of these dissimilarities contain apparent contradictions? Or could the similarities be explained by appeal to a massive oral tradition which had preserved both the narrative and the discourse materials so exactly that separate authors borrowing independently from this oral tradition could produce the phenomena which exist (thus Herder and Gieseler)? Professional storytellers in non-literary cultures are able to achieve remarkable results in transmitting stories from generation to generation with a high degree of verbal fixity. But was the tradition in the earliest Christian community perpetuated by such professional storytellers? Above all, how does it happen that the verbal agreements here under consideration are in the Greek text, while the original tradition concerning Jesus must have begun as an Aramaic oral tradition? How could the translation of an Aramaic oral tradition into Greek have been controlled so as to produce an unwritten *textus receptus* widely available and used independently by the authors of Matthew, Mark, and Luke? The conviction emerged that only some form of dependence at the level of the written tradition could explain the striking verbal similarities in Greek between the Synoptics. (Note the striking phrase in Matt. 24:15c and Mark 13:14b, "Let the *reader* understand. . . .") But had there been a single primitive gospel, an *Urevangelium,* from which all three evangelists borrowed (Lessing), or had many small written fragments been in circulation to be variously arranged by the Synoptic writers (Schleiermacher), or, finally, had one of our Gospels been used by the others (Griesbach)?

The results of this period of intensive research are well-known. In 1838 two men working independently, Christian Gottlob Wilke, a Protestant minister turning Roman Catholic, and Christian H. Weisse, a professor of philosophy, both came to the conclusion that Mark was the earliest of the Synoptics and that it had been used as a source both by Matthew and by Luke.[6] This assumption of the priority of Mark and of its use by Matthew and Luke is now overwhelmingly though not quite universally accepted.[7] For a considerable period it was opposed by Roman Catholic scholars largely because of the second-century tradition which made a Hebrew (or Aramaic) version of Matthew the earliest Gospel. However, many Roman Catholic scholars now agree that our present Greek Matthew is clearly dependent on Mark, as is Luke.

We saw previously that the fourth stage in the handling of the sources emerged with the two-source theory of the Synoptic Gospels. Obviously Mark was one of these two sources. But what of the other? Once it was agreed that Matthew and Luke had used Mark it was possible to attribute to Mark the similar materials in Matthew or Luke. But upon further investigation it became clear that there were still curious agreements between Matthew and Luke outside the area of their common dependence on Mark. The most commonly accepted explanation was that Matthew and Luke, in addition to using Mark, had also shared a second source which consisted primarily of sayings of Jesus. This hypothetical second source was christened "Q," presumably an abbreviation of the German word for "source" (*Quelle*). Generally speaking

---

[6] The work of Wilke and Weisse is summarized in Schweitzer, *op. cit.*, chapter 10.

[7] The most recent major study challenging the priority of Mark is that of W. R. Farmer, *The Synoptic Problem: A Critical Analysis* (New York: Macmillan, 1964).

"Q" was used to describe either the material which Matthew and Luke had in common apart from the Marcan material, or else it was used to identify a written document from which this material was believed to have been borrowed. There have been periodic protests against the "Q" hypothesis, and at present Austin Farrar of Oxford spearheads such a protest. Yet most of the work on the Quest for the historical Jesus done over the past century has been on the assumption that Matthew and Luke used both Mark and a "Q" source. Additional hypotheses have grown up around these, but they are not crucial for the overall development.

At this fourth stage of the development the tendency was for the sources to be reduced to Mark and "Q." Admittedly there was considerable material both in Matthew and Luke which did not come from these two sources and which, theoretically, might have been derived from sources—written or oral—as early or as authentic as either Mark or "Q." But it was psychologically natural for scholars to think of Mark and "Q" as the basic sources and to use the special materials of Matthew or Luke only in a secondary or provisional way. B. H. Streeter attempted to give these homeless materials a home by proposing two additional sources "M" and "L," the former being the source for much of Matthew's distinctive material while the latter fulfilled the same function in relation to Luke.[8] Streeter's views were supported by carefully detailed arguments, and they received considerable acceptance in Britain. Elsewhere they have received more respect than acceptance, perhaps partly because in Europe the center of attention in Gospel studies had already moved elsewhere. It is obvious that the farther one moves from Mark, which unquestionably exists, the more speculative the hypotheses become. However, at the turn of the century Mark and "Q" were the generally recognized sources, Mark providing the framework for the ministry and "Q" contributing the bulk of the teaching.

[8] B. H. Streeter, *The Four Gospels* (rev. ed.; London: Macmillan, 1930).

It is obvious that as New Testament research moved through the four stages just described there was a steady reduction of the material regarded as primary source material for the reconstruction of the ministry of Jesus. First it had been the New Testament, then the four Gospels, then the three Synoptics, and finally the two sources behind the Synoptics, Mark and "Q." In the twentieth century we have moved to a *fifth stage,* which is more complicated than any two previous ones. Two factors contributed to the emergence of this fifth period. One may be described by reference to the work of Wilhelm Wrede on the Gospel of Mark, while the other is the "form criticism" associated particularly with the names of Martin Dibelius, Rudolf Bultmann, and Karl Ludwig Schmidt.

In 1901 Wrede published a book whose title may be translated as "The Messianic Secret in the Gospels."[9] It was a direct challenge to the current assumptions concerning Mark, the earliest narrative source for the ministry of Jesus. It had been taken for granted that this source was essentially historical in the ordinary sense of that term. It is true that the so-called "liberal movement" had had a fondness for eliminating the supernatural element from the tradition while taking the "natural" elements at their face value, as if the Christian community, once it set out to create stories about Jesus, would confine its creativity to the production of strictly supernatural stories. But in general the scholars of the period accepted the pattern of the ministry they claimed to find in Mark. Wrede contended that the incongruities in Mark could be explained only when it was understood that the entire Gospel had been written with a deliberate theological purpose, that it was, if you will, a deliberate rewrite job in the light of the theological convictions which had arisen after the resurrection. The incongruities which Wrede alleged centered around the

---

[9] *Das Messiasgeheimnis in den Evangelien: zugleich ein Beitrag zum Verständnis des Markusevangeliums* (Göttingen: Vandenhoeck and Ruprecht, 1901; reissued, Vandenhoeck and Ruprecht, 1963).

"Messianic secret." According to the Gospel of Mark as it now stands, Jesus was and knew himself to be the Messiah. As such he performed miracles, was acclaimed by the demon-possessed, and revealed his Messiahship to his disciples. But somehow his public ministry went on as if no such claim had been made. The Messianic question never became a source of controversy. Wrede contended that the Messianic motif originated only with the Resurrection, and that the Christian community, speaking through Mark, projected this motif back into the earthly ministry of Jesus. Since the actual record did not express the motif it was necessary to introduce it everywhere as a secret.

We are not concerned with the details or the validity of Wrede's argument. It was important because it challenged the accepted conviction that if scholars could get back to the earliest written source they would then be in almost direct touch with the ministry of Jesus. Wrede suggested that the road back ended in the life of the earliest community, and that while that community remembered the events of Jesus' ministry it remembered them in the transforming light of Good Friday and Easter. The history had been "theologized," enormously complicating historical research.

The focus of Wrede on the creative role of the community in the transformation of the tradition about Jesus was greatly intensified after World War I by the emergence of form criticism (*Formgeschichte*). It was agreed that a generation had elapsed between the end of Jesus' earthly ministry and the appearance of the written sources. Thus far Gospel criticism had dealt chiefly with these written sources. Was it possible by some type of analysis or speculation to determine what had happened to the tradition between A.D. 30 and 60, the so-called "tunnel period," or "the period of the oral tradition"? The form critics began by noting that the narrative in Mark does not read like a single, consecutive narrative. It is rather a series of vignettes linked together by connecting phrases but not organically related. If a particular incident is extracted the narrative does not "bleed." From this the form critics concluded that the stories about Jesus had circulated as independent units in the Christian community before being combined in Mark or in still earlier sources. It was agreed that the passion narrative must have been the earliest consecutive narrative since it is the section most difficult to dissolve into separate units.

The form critics contended further that these isolated stories had circulated widely in the Christian community, being used over and over in response to the practical needs of that community, namely, preaching, teaching, controversy, and exhortation. It was also argued that when stories circulate from mouth to mouth they tend to fall into certain definite patterns or shapes. We need not be concerned with the particular "forms" which the form critics claimed to be able to identify but rather with the fact that in their discussions of the changes of "forms" they became involved in the further question of the change in the *content* of the stories as they were repeated and adapted by the community to the needs of a particular situation. The question also arose as to the kind of community in which a particular "form" of story was shaped or created. Bultmann, probably the most distinguished and most radical expert in this specialized area, claimed to be able to distinguish between "forms" which arose in Palestinian communities and others which arose in Hellenistic communities. Naturally his disciples were soon able to make the same distinctions. Obviously this type of analysis went far beyond the classification of literary "forms"; it endeavored to provide a base for determining whether stories were early or late appearances in the tradition. The ordinary Bible reader who plunges unwarily into the world of Bultmann and his disciples finds himself totally confused amid the apparently arbitrary and frequently negative judgments passed on stories long accepted as direct pictures of events during the ministry of Jesus. But such an estimate of the form critics is not entirely fair. There is a pattern, a system, by which they carry out their work. Admittedly it contains some elements of the subjective, and only time will tell whether this technique is equal to the claims which have been made for it.

III

However form criticism is finally evaluated, it is clear that in the hands of Bultmann and of others equally radical it created a new situation. Previously there had been a reduction of the sources to be used for the recovery of the historical Jesus; now there was an evaporation of those sources. To put it less extremely, the Gospels remained as sources, but they were sources primarily for the life of the early church. It was believed that the skilled expert could move back behind the records, in some cases back even to Jesus himself. But the operation is so delicate that differences of opinion may always exist as to the way in which it should be carried out. Furthermore, a haunting question remains: Even if the later strata of the tradition can be removed, will what emerges reflect the historical Jesus or, perhaps, only an earlier stage of the tradition? To change the metaphor, the Gospels are now regarded, by Bultmann and most good form critics, as palimpsests in which the faith of the early community has been written heavily over the tradition of Jesus himself. Can the two layers, or, perhaps, the three or four layers, be separated? Will we know if we reach the bottom layer? Is the bottom layer the historical Jesus?

Before saying anything further about Bultmann, who is the storm center in the current discussion about the possibility and the legitimacy of the Quest for the historical Jesus, we must go back to the end of the nineteenth century to comment on a document which created comparatively little interest then but which subsequently became important. In 1892 Martin Kähler, a professor of theology in Halle, Germany, published a lecture with the somewhat paradoxical title, *Der sogennante, historische Jesus und der geschichtliche, biblische Christus.*[10] It is difficult to translate this title since it uses two different German words for "historical" (*historisch* and *geschichtlich*) which do not have precise parallels in English. In Carl E. Braaten's translation[11] the two terms have been rendered by "historical" and "historic," respectively, on the premise that the former more naturally refers to the purely external facticity of an event while the latter term points toward its significance and meaning. Kähler's contemporaries who were engaged in the Quest for the historical Jesus took it largely for granted that the recovery of the Jesus *behind* the Gospels would result in a purification and strengthening of the Christian faith. The Jesus of history would serve as norm for the Christ of faith. Or, to put it a little more strongly, the Christ of faith as distinct from the Jesus of history would disappear, and the Jesus of history alone would be the guide for Christian life and faith.

Kähler took the position that, at best, historical research could recover only a portion of the whole reality, and that in the case of Jesus this result was even less satisfactory than usual in view of the nature of the documents and of the uniqueness of Jesus who, as the Word made flesh, could not be interpreted by ordinary techniques. On the positive side he held that the object of Christian faith was not the earthly Jesus, who could be only partially and uncertainly recovered by historical research, but the total, biblical Christ, who was everywhere proclaimed on the pages of the New Testament. When the Word became flesh it was the "Word" that constituted the revelation and not the "flesh" per se. The "Word" was heard and repeated by the apostles and is directly available to us. Kähler agreed entirely with those who asserted that the early church's remembrance of

---

[10] Leipzig: A. Deichert. It was reissued, with another, introductory essay prefixed, in 1896.

[11] Martin Kähler, *The So-called Historical Jesus and the Historic, Biblical Christ*, trans. and ed. Carl E. Braaten (Philadelphia: Fortress, 1964). See especially pp. 20–21.

Jesus was colored by the experience of Good Friday and Easter and the ongoing awareness of the resurrected Christ. But he insisted that this did not result in a discoloration or distortion of Jesus' earthly ministry; indeed this coloration brought out the true significance of his ministry. It brought into focus the ultimate meaning of Christ's life, death, and resurrection. Kähler's language was not always clear, and this may reflect confusions in his own thought, but the central thrust of his position is unmistakeable. The real Christ in the ultimate sense is to be encountered in the pages of the New Testament and in the preaching which continues the apostolic proclamation. The simple Christian does not need to stand, cap in hand, at the study door of the professor of historical research awaiting the latest pronouncement concerning the historical Jesus. Professor and simple Christian are on a par as they read the pages of the New Testament or as they listen to the contemporary proclamation of Christ.

In many ways the thought of Bultmann and his associates parallels that of Kähler. Two clear differences must be noted, however. *First,* for Bultmann the acids of criticism have eaten more deeply into the sources than Kähler would have assumed and, as a result, the tension between "the so-called historical Jesus" and "the historic, biblical Christ" is much greater than any nineteenth-century thinker imagined. *Secondly,* Bultmann's project of "demythologizing" has carried him into a far more radical position vis-à-vis the Christ of faith than Kähler would have found acceptable. While Bultmann does not deny that something can be known about the historical Jesus through the tedious and uncertain process of historical research, he assumes that comparatively little can be known and that only with relative certainty. Yet he is not troubled theologically about this situation. For him the object of Christian faith is the resurrected and exalted Christ proclaimed in the kerygma of the New Testament and of the continuing community. It is here that we encounter the living Word of God that is able to transform our lives and to open us to the future which comes to us from God as gift and as grace. Admittedly Bultmann's program of demythologizing is so extreme that the content which he gives to the phrase "the resurrected and exalted Christ" may seem entirely unsatisfactory. But this must not confuse the central point he is making, namely, that Christian faith is directed, not toward the historical details of the human Jesus, but toward the Christ of faith. Even those who are chilled by his radical criticism are warmed by the evangelical note which enters his teaching and preaching at this point. The historical Jesus must be subordinated in order that the Christ of faith may be exalted. Whenever Bultmann observes an intense concern for the Jesus of history, he is immediately suspicious that the individuals involved are attempting to prove faith by the details of history. For Bultmann this a fatuous endeavor. Any theological concern for the Quest for the historical Jesus falls under the condemnation of II Corinthians 5:16: ". . . even though we once regarded Christ from a human point of view, we regard him thus no longer." Faith is the response to the proclaimed Christ, and the amassing of historical footnotes about his earthly ministry will not establish faith. It has even been suggested that Bultmann's enthusiasm for the most radical expressions of Gospel criticism is unconsciously motivated by his desire to destroy what he regards as a false foundation or false support for faith.

The most obvious and frequent charge against Bultmann is that he seems so to separate the resurrected Christ from the earthly Jesus that docetism is a natural if not intended result. Instead of "The Word became flesh," Bultmann proclaims "The Word became kerygma. . . ." Certainly Bultmann insists that there is a continuity between the earthly ministry of Jesus and the Christ proclaimed in the kerygma, but the kerygma is very far from being identical with the teaching of the earthly Jesus. We can be sure of the *Dass* but not of the *Was* of the historical Jesus— of the "that" (he lived and taught) but not of the "what" (the details of his life and ministry). But if this is correct, does it not mean that there is no essential relation between the kerygma and the kind or quality of life through which it came into the world? Is it only accidental, or incidental, that the kerygma is linked with Jesus of Nazareth rather than with Judas Iscariot or Pontius Pilate? This is not to say that the quality of life ascribed to Jesus *proves* the kerygma to be of God. But it does mean that there should be some congruity between the "Word" and the "flesh" if the concept of incarnation—however interpreted—is to have any meaning. If the "Word" and the "flesh" were not only distinct but also opposite in the incarnation then the term "incarnation" is a misnomer.

It is easy to raise questions concerning Bultmann's position, but such questions must be examined in the light of the counterquestions which Bultmann directs toward his critics. However, these problems must be postponed until the final chapter, when various possibilities will be considered.

IV

Particular stress has been laid on Bultmann's position both because of its own interest and because alternative views are most easily understood by their relation to the Bultmann pattern. In a brief survey of the present situation it will be appropriate to comment first on those scholars who stand in the Bultmann tradition and then on others who dissent from his views. The Bultmann disciples share his general approach, but it is significant that in the past decade they have displayed varying degrees of dissatisfaction at the implied abandonment of the Quest for the historical Jesus. This dissatisfaction has given rise to the movement described as "A New Quest of the Historical Jesus." The most convenient presentation of the background of this movement is to be found in the book by James M. Robinson bearing that title,[12] while the most concrete result of the movement ap-

---

[12] *A New Quest of the Historical Jesus* ("Studies in Biblical Theology," No. 25; London: SCM, 1959). An expanded, German version has also appeared.

pears in Günther Bornkamm's *Jesus of Nazareth,* which was translated into English in 1960. Half a dozen other New Testament scholars, chiefly in Germany, have been prominent in this movement, and Professor Bultmann paid his respects to them in a lecture at Heidelberg University in 1959.[13]

In general the members of this group agree that it is impossible to argue from history to faith, that the Gospels are heavily colored by the postresurrection beliefs and by subsequent developments in the Palestinian or Hellenistic Christian communities, and that the essential kerygma may be recovered from the pages of the New Testament quite apart from the rediscovery of the historical Jesus through modern research. But they are also conscious of the danger of docetism inherent in Bultmann's formulations of his position, and they are eager to develop "A New Quest" at least as a symbol of their concern for the historical Jesus.

Bornkamm's first chapter begins with the sentence, "No one is any longer in the position to write a life of Jesus." Later, on the same page, he states that we are compelled "to affirm the futility of any renewal of attempts at Lives of Jesus now or in the future." These sentences do not mean what the uninitiated reader might imagine, since if they did the book would necessarily end with its beginning. Bornkamm meant, as he was careful to explain, that it is no longer thought possible to write a life of Jesus in which there is a clear chronological sequence or a tracing of the inner and outer developments of the ministry. Nevertheless Bornkamm affirms that we are not cut off from the historical Jesus. "Our task, then, is to seek the history *in* the Kerygma of the Gospels, and in this history to seek the Kerygma" (p. 21). He contended that despite the overwriting of the individual in-

[13] *Das Verhältnis der urchristlichen Christusbotschaft zum historichen Jesus* (Heidelberg: Carl Winter, 1961). The essay has now been translated in Carl E. Braaten and Roy A. Harrisville (eds.), *The Historical Jesus and the Kerygmatic Christ* (New York: Abingdon, 1964).

cidents in the light of the postresurrection events there is an "authenticity," a "freshness," and a "distinctiveness" which "points us directly to the earthly figure of Jesus" (p. 24). Rightly understood, "the primitive tradition of Jesus is brim full of history" (p. 26). Since I am primarily concerned with basic methodology and attitude rather than with the results of their application, I leave Bornkamm at this point with the recommendation that the book itself be read. Perhaps the footnote should be added that Bornkamm began his book with an *apologia* and that this is characteristic of the mood that has emerged since the development of form criticism. Indeed, even those who reject major aspects of the full creed of form criticism and who continue their Quest along older lines feel obliged to defend and explain their procedures over against the problems raised by Bultmann.

Probably James M. Robinson is the American most closely associated with the developments growing out of Bultmann's position. In the introductory section of *A New Quest of the Historical Jesus* he deals with "The Impossibility and Illegitimacy of the Original Quest." He contends that it was impossible because the sources do not provide the necessary information. They were affirmations of faith rather than historical resource material. The Quest, in its original form, was illegitimate because it believed that the recovery of the externals of the ministry of Jesus could serve as a foundation and norm for faith. In the remaining three chapters he deals with the "Possibility," the "Legitimacy," and the "Procedure" of a *New* Quest. A New Quest, he argues, is possible and even necessary because of developments in modern, scientific historiography. Faith is not and cannot be dependent upon historiography, but the rise of modern historiography has exposed the distinction between the kerygma and the historical Jesus. Once this distinction has been made clear it becomes necessary to show that the kerygma is not "symbolized principle" but "interpreted history" (p. 81). Or again, "The Kerygma is not the objectification of a new 'Christian' religious principle, but

rather the objectification of a historical encounter with God"
(p. 84). This New Quest, even if successful, cannot prove the
ultimate truth of the kerygma, but it can "test whether this kerygmatic understanding of Jesus' existence corresponds to the understanding of existence implicit in Jesus' history" (p. 94). In
more commonplace language, he is contending that a New Quest
should be able to show whether the message of the church is
commensurate with the message of Jesus' own life and teaching.
The most startling feature of Robinson's argument is his suggestion that a New Quest conducted on the lines of a new historiography could produce an encounter with the historical Jesus
in which the kerygmatic significance of Jesus would be as visible
as it is in the Gospels as they stand (p. 95). This new doctrine
of the "Two Ways"—both good—has met some resistance or at
least skepticism.

But why does Robinson believe that such a New Quest is possible in the light of the difficulties which, according to the Bultmann school, inevitably frustrated the previous Quest? Robinson
believes that the changed understanding of history associated with
the names of Wilhelm Dilthey and R. G. Collingwood has revealed possibilities not open to nineteenth-century historiography
which specialized in "historicism" and "psychologism." According to Robinson we now understand that, in the final analysis,
"History is the act of intention, the commitment, the meaning
for the participants, behind the external occurrence" (p. 67).
He feels that this aspect of the ministry of Jesus can be recovered
despite the modifications which the church introduced into much
of the tradition. Presumably Robinson means that despite the
thoroughgoing transformation of the tradition some sayings or
incidents still shine through from the original Jesus. While this
limited number of incidents would be totally inadequate for the
creation of a "Life" in the fashion of nineteenth-century historiography, it does provide enough material for the new historiography to determine what was really essential about the Jesus of

history, namely, the "act of intention, the commitment" which stood behind all of his actions.

I must confess to some doubts at this point. It is clear that the collapse of confidence in the chronological sequence of Gospel events is far more harmful for nineteenth-century historiography than for the proponents of the newer version. But when the new historiographer turns his attention to the isolated incident he is confronted with the same problems that pursued his predecessor, namely, how it is possible to strip off the layers of later tradition and to determine whether the earliest layer truly reflects the historical Jesus. That this may be done in some cases even Bultmann agrees. But can it be done with enough confidence, and in enough cases, to allow a firm conclusion concerning the overall "act of intention" behind Jesus' ministry? Probably only further testing and further discussion will permit a reasonable answer to this question. Is it possible to understand Jesus' "act of intention" without a clear understanding of what the concepts "kingdom of God" and "Son of man" meant to him, or without knowing how he viewed his impending death? Is this information available at present?

The most homogeneous group of scholars standing over against Bultmann and the post-Bultmannians is a group representing what may be called, with a little oversimplification, the "British viewpoint."[14] While this persuasion is not confined to those from Britain or even to those from the British Commonwealth it is represented in distinguished fashion by men such as C. H. Dodd, T. W. Manson, W. D. Davies, and Vincent Taylor. While these men genuflect in the direction of form criticism, it is quite clear that they do not share the more radical opinions which are fashionable in those circles. They explicitly avoid language about a "New Quest" and prefer to speak of the original Quest as "resumed" or "continued." They are puzzled or even irritated by

---

[14] Some of the material in the following paragraphs has already appeared in my article, "Basic Issues," *Interpretation*, XVIII, 1 (January, 1964), 39–55.

the "extremes" which they detect, particularly among some German scholars. In the fall of 1961 I attended two conferences in Great Britain which brought together a considerable number of British, American, and Continental scholars in the biblical field. The most obvious division of opinion was that between the "British" and the Bultmannian points of view.

C. H. Dodd has utilized many of the insights of form criticism. However, in a famous article, "The Framework of the Gospel Narrative," in the *Expository Times* of June, 1932, he argued that along with isolated stories the early Christian community handed down also an outline of the ministry, an outline which, according to Dodd, is reflected essentially in the "summaries" of Mark's Gospel. If this is correct then the basic chronological outline of the ministry is discernible and considerably more may be said about the "Life" of Jesus than the Bultmann school concedes. Again in 1938 Dodd published a series of lectures under the title *History and the Gospel*.[15] Here it became even more clear that for Dodd the veil between the reader of the Gospels and the Jesus of history is comparatively thin. By stressing the recurrence of similar motifs in the various "sources" of the (Synoptic) Gospels and in the various "forms," he believes it is possible to establish a fairly clearcut picture of the ministry and message of Jesus.[16]

In the mid-1940's T. W. Manson published a series of lectures in the Bulletin of the John Rylands Library under the title, *The Life of Jesus: A Study of the Available Materials*. These have now been conveniently published, along with others of his writings, in the volume *Studies in the Gospels and Epistles*.[17] In this new form the series is introduced by a lecture from 1949, "The Quest of the Historical Jesus—Continued," which includes a number of sharp pronouncements against the position of Bult-

[15] New York: Scribner, 1938.

[16] See especially chap. 3, "Historical Criticism of the Gospels," and chap. 4, "The Gospel Story."

[17] Manchester University Press, 1962.

mann and his associates. In the other lectures dealing with the Gospels he argues that a substantial portion of Mark is Petrine material repeated by John Mark and that the hypothetical "Q" document was written by Matthew the Apostle. These conclusions, he contends, justify the assumption that the Synoptics contain a decisive amount of what is practically eyewitness material. Manson's concern for the question of authorship distinguishes him from the form critics who regard the Gospel materials as versions of community tradition. In an earlier work Manson had argued that a careful study of Mark's vocabulary and style supports the thesis that the ministry of Jesus was actually divided into two halves by the confession of Peter at Caesarea Philippi.[18] Furthermore, using the multiple sources as multiple witnesses for particular motifs in the teaching of Jesus, Manson recreated with considerable confidence various aspects of Jesus' original message.

A similar confidence in our ability to recapture the basic outline and message of the historical Jesus has been displayed both by Vincent Taylor[19] and W. D. Davies. The latter gave his inaugural address at Union Theological Seminary, in 1959, the provocative title, "A Quest to be Resumed in New Testament Studies," thus disassociating himself from those who insist on a new and different Quest.[20]

But the British are not alone in their opposition to Bultmann. Scandinavian scholars, who have long been concerned with the whole question of oral tradition, have argued that the form critics are right in suggesting that the material in the Gospels is community tradition but that they are wrong in assuming that this tradition was handed on without careful controls. On the contrary, say these scholars, the tradition was transmitted with

[18] T. W. Manson, *The Teaching of Jesus* (2nd ed.; Cambridge University Press, 1935).

[19] Vincent Taylor, *The Life and Ministry of Jesus* (Nashville: Abingdon, 1955).

[20] The address has been included in Davies' recent volume, *Christian Origins and Judaism* (Philadelphia: Westminster, 1962).

great care, as was the Rabbinic tradition of the same period. This protest against the conclusions of the Bultmann school was made by Harald Riesenfeld at the International Congress on the Four Gospels held at Oxford in 1957.[21] It has been developed in more detail in a doctoral dissertation by Birger Gerhardsson.[22]

In Germany itself Joachim Jeremias and Ethelbert Stauffer have been consistent opponents of Bultmann. Jeremias, an expert in Aramaic studies and in the Jewish background of the New Testament, contends that the kerygma itself requires the recovery of the Jesus of history if faith is to have a firm foundation. He is undaunted by the admittedly absurd portraits which emerged during the nineteenth century and feels that the erraticisms of the earlier Quest can be eliminated as historical techniques are sharpened and new materials accumulate. The ministry of Jesus and the response of the community belong together, but it is the historical ministry which must have the priority: ". . . Jesus of Nazareth is God's call to his creatures; confession of him is their response. This response . . . is inspired by the Spirit of God, but it does not take the place of the call. The call, not the response, is the decisive thing."[23] Jeremias is famous for his analyses of the Semitic terms "Abba" and "Amen," which he believes were used by Jesus in so distinctive a fashion that they reflect the essence of Jesus' own Christology, the one term expressing a unique intimacy with God, the other a unique authority.[24]

The extreme reaction of Stauffer to the Bultmann position may be seen by English readers in his book *Jesus and His Story*.[25] In

[21] Harald Riesenfeld, *The Gospel Tradition and Its Beginnings: A Study in the Limits of Formgeschichte* (London: Mowbray, 1957).

[22] *Memory and Manuscript* (Lund: Gleerup, 1961).

[23] Joachim Jeremias, *The Problem of the Historical Jesus*, trans. Norman Perrin ("Facet Books—Biblical Series," No. 13; Philadelphia: Fortress, 1964), p. 23.

[24] See his contribution to *Synoptische Studien: Alfred Wikenhauser zum siebzigsten Geburtstag* (Munich: K. Zink, 1953), "Kennzeichen der ipsissima vox Jesu"; see now also his *The Lord's Prayer*, trans. John Reumann ("Facet Books—Biblical Series," No. 8; Philadelphia: Fortress, 1964).

[25] Trans. Richard and Clara Winston (New York: Knopf, 1960).

the Preface Stauffer recognizes the problems that frustrated the older Quest, but he insists that new sources permit victory over that frustration. Strictly speaking, he does not mean new types of sources but rather an accumulation of the old sources, chiefly sources which portray the milieu in which Jesus lived and worked. In this respect Stauffer resembles Jeremias, but Stauffer has been far less cautious in his handling of the materials and in his conclusions. He has attracted considerable attention by his "conservative" judgments on the historicity of items both in the Synoptics and in John, but it must be said that the fraternity of New Testament scholars looks with some suspicion at the way in which he jumps from information about first-century customs to specific conclusions about events in the life of Jesus. Whether this suspicion reflects more on Stauffer or on the fraternity of New Testament scholars will remain for time to judge—though some are not waiting!

Thus, for some the Quest is regarded as theologically unimportant if not actually dangerous (Bultmann); for others it is important but it must be carried out in a new way (the post-Bultmannians); while for still others the Quest continues as before, although there are sharpened techniques and additional materials to bring to the task.

Before closing this survey it may be helpful to underline three items which have been implicit in this discussion of the developments during the past two centuries but which need direct statement.

First, while the twentieth-century Quest has emerged out of the one which began in the eighteenth century, it is, in a certain sense, looking in a very different direction. The eighteenth-century Quest began with the assumption of a tension between the Jesus of history and the Christ of faith, the concern being to discover a Jesus of history who would be *other than* that Christ of faith. In other words, the Quest at that point was concerned to document the *discontinuity* between the Jesus of history and the Christ of faith. Today, where the Quest continues or begins as a New Quest, there is an attempt to discover the *continuity* between the Jesus of history and the Christ of faith—or at least to demonstrate a congruity between these two entities.

Second, while the earlier Quest began and was carried out by the more radical wing of the Christian community, it has been taken over by those representing a more conservative position. In a real sense the radical wing (Bultmann) is no longer concerned with the Quest, that is, insofar as theology is concerned. But the more conservative scholars, who at one time viewed the entire process with skepticism, are now busily engaged with the questions which the radical groups seem to be abandoning.

Third, while there is a marked difference between those who are optimistic and those who are pessimistic about the recovery of the Jesus of history, both positions serve to bring into the foreground a central theological problem, namely, how is the certainty of faith to be related to the uncertainties of historical research? From the perspective of the historian there is a significant difference between those who claim to be ninety percent certain of what they "know" about the historical Jesus and those who are only seventy percent certain. Similarly there is a difference between those who purport to know only a few facts and those who are prepared to write a fairly detailed biography. But the discussions of the past half-century have made it clear that these controversies are at the level of greater and lesser degrees of probability. They do not rise to the level of certainty. The problem of the relation between historical probability and the certainty of faith remains whether one is persuaded by the skepticism of Bultmann or by the optimism of the British. This is the real problem which craves an answer.

6

Principles
and
Persuasions

In this final chapter it is my hazardous task to come out from the shelter of historical description and to state my convictions concerning the Quest for the historical Jesus and its implications for faith. I begin with five propositions about biblical history and history in general. These constitute the background for my own thinking.

I

First Proposition. Biblical history is not inerrant history. For some this is so obvious as not to require statement, while for others this view is so erroneous that all subsequent statements must also be erroneous. The implications of this proposition are serious. It means that the ostensibly historical accounts in the Bible, whether of the exodus or of Jesus' ministry, are not to be accepted automatically as literal history in the ordinary sense of that phrase. For the present purpose it does not matter whether one is as radical as Bultmann or as conservative as Stauffer. Both agree that biblical history is not inerrant history. It must therefore be investigated by the usual techniques of research. Using the terminology of the first chapter, there is a tension between the record and the history, and we can work back from the record

toward the history only by the use of historical research. Differences of opinion respecting the proportion of the material
regarded as probably historical do not affect the central problem
with which we are concerned or the theological difficulties created by this problem.

There are modern theologians and historians who still insist
that the biblical history is inerrant. With all due respect for such
individuals I can state only that from my perspective they seem
to escape the evidence against inerrancy in one or both of two
illegitimate ways. Either they discuss the concept of inerrancy
in the abstract so that the concrete problems which arise, for example, from a comparison of the Synoptic Gospels, do not appear
in their studies; or, alternatively, when they discuss specific problems their interpretation of the concept of inerrancy suddenly,
and unexpectedly, becomes so elastic that one is no longer able
to recognize it as inerrancy.

If one believes in inerrancy in spite of these difficulties, then
the problem of historical certainty has been solved. But for the
rest of us the problem remains.

Second Proposition. Historical research in biblical as in secular
history produces only probability results. It is possible to achieve
substantial certainty concerning some aspects of the careers of
public individuals from the ancient past provided they lived in
periods for which public or diversified private records are available. We may know a good deal, with practical certainty, about
Alexander the Great or Julius Caesar. But even what we know
of them is not known with absolute certainty. And when we
turn from the more external aspects of their careers to inquire
concerning their characters, their intentions, their motives, there
is a marked decrease in the confidence with which we can accept
the answers given. We have the slightly cynical feeling that if
there were more scholars devoting their talents to investigating
these aspects of Alexander or Caesar there would be a greater
diversity in the portraits we would receive of them.

Perhaps some individuals are unaware of this element of uncertainty hovering around historical judgments. The dates and other externals can be established with overwhelming certainty—sometimes. But any attempt to state the inner sequence or the significance of events leads to diversity of opinion. This is obvious to anyone who attempts to investigate the causes of World War I, to take an obvious illustration. Relevant and documented information is available in enormous quantities. Eyewitnesses and participants are still among us. But it can scarcely be said that a universally convincing evaluation of the causes has yet been achieved. I remember an encyclopedia which evaded the problem by presenting two articles on "The Causes of the World War," one from a French scholar and the other from a German. In such matters a single, unified interpretation may emerge with the passing of time. But in part this acquiescence in a single theory is the result of a diminution of interest in the question. Why worry about the causes of World War I when the investigator has World War II to analyze, not to mention a potential World War III? Of course, a few professionals continue to discuss the old question. But dissenting voices die out, the public ceases to be concerned, the echoes of the last, loud voice reverberate around the world. Only unread doctoral theses dispute details of the accepted and conventional interpretation.

Geoffrey Barraclough in *History in a Changing World* (p. 14) wrote, "The history we read, though based on facts, is, strictly speaking, not factual at all, but a series of accepted judgments." This quotation is taken from the delightful first chapter of E. H. Carr's book, *What is History?*[1] I recommend this chapter to anyone unaware of the degree of subjectivity involved in the accepted "facts" of history.

We said earlier that it is possible to achieve substantial certainty concerning some aspects of the careers of public persons.

[1] New York: Knopf, 1962

Jesus of Nazareth was not a public person in this sense. Or, at best, he was a public person only at the time of his crucifixion. For that aspect of his career there are no extant public records, though some in the early church attempted to rectify this situation by "producing" such public records. The records which we do have, basically the four Gospels, cannot be described as diversified, private records. They represent in various ways the traditions concerning Jesus which were perpetuated by those who believed in him, that is to say, those who remembered his earthly ministry from the transforming perspective of the Easter experiences. They were those who when they spoke of his earthly ministry were also witnessing to their resurrected and present Lord. This complicates the task of disentangling the one from the other, the accounts of the earthly ministry from the witness to the risen Lord. Furthermore, these Gospels are anonymous documents, although second-century tradition attached the names of specific individuals to each of the four. The traditions concerning authorship have greater and lesser degrees of probability. Unfortunately for historical research the lesser degrees of probability apply to the first and fourth Gospels, i.e., precisely those Gospels which were attributed to eyewitnesses of the ministry of Jesus.

This does not mean that the Gospels are necessarily inaccurate in any substantial way. It does mean that the research expert lacks the controls over his sources which he needs in order to estimate the degrees of probability in any given instance. I remind you of a statement which is not from Rudolf Bultmann but from Archbishop Temple: ". . . there is no single deed or saying of which we can be perfectly sure that He said or did precisely this or that."[2]

By way of a brief digression may I point out that even Bultmann is confident we know some things about the actual career of

---

[2] William Temple, in *Revelation,* ed. J. Baillie and H. Martin (London: Macmillan, 1937), p. 114.

Jesus. In all likelihood he performed exorcisms, violated Sabbath regulations and the prescriptions concerning "clean" and "unclean," attacked Jewish legalism, associated with religious and social outcasts as well as with women and children. It is also probable that, unlike John, he was not an ascetic. He called on men to follow him and gathered a band of followers including both men and women. He announced the imminence of the kingdom of God.[3] Many of us who are not as "skeptical" as Bultmann would confidently add a considerable number of items to this list. But none of this changes the second proposition, namely, that historical research in biblical as in secular history produces only probability results.

Third Proposition. The pictures of the past which historical research is able to establish on the basis of probability evidence are always *less* than the reality of the original events. To risk a grisly analogy, the researcher is like one who attempts to describe a man's life from the post-mortem examination of his "remains." And the "remains" are normally incomplete. This limitation on historical research is inherent in the nature of history itself. A total picture of an event requires the recall of all the details involved. Such total recall is impossible once the event has passed out of the present to become a part of the past. An adequate portrait may be based on the recall of a part of the details connected with the original event. But the accuracy of such a portrait could be demonstrated with certainty only if all the details were recalled for such a verification—and it is not quite certain it could be demonstrated even then. The more the researcher confines himself to the details which can be recalled with substantial probability the more limited is his presentation of the original event. The more he supplements the details which can be recalled with substantial probability—in an effort to recapture

[3] Bultmann gave this brief summary in the lecture referred to in the previous chapter, *Das Verhältnis der urchristlichen Christusbotschaft zum Historichen Jesus.*

the totality of the original—the more risk there is of distortion. Thus there is an inevitable gap between the demonstrable probability about an event and its original reality. The mere chronicler may be content to present the demonstrable probability, i.e., the externals of an event which protrude sufficiently above the stream of history to be visible to subsequent generations farther down that stream. But one who is not a mere chronicler must add something of his own if these dry bones are to live.

Applied to the Quest for the historical Jesus this means that whatever can be *proved* by research about the ministry of Jesus is and will always be less than the original reality experienced by the community. This would be true even if there were substantial agreement among the scholars as to what can be proved. Here the whole is more than the sum of all its parts, and a part is certainly less than the sum of the parts. At best only a part can be known of the historical Jesus by means of historical research.

I have already pointed out that from the perspective of research our sources are not ideal. They appear as written documents a generation or more after the close of Jesus' earthly career. They are anonymous documents. They were written in Greek while the language of Jesus and his earliest disciples was primarily Aramaic. More important than the shift from one language to another is that this shift indicates that the Gospels were written at a considerable geographical and cultural distance from the original Palestinian community in which the events occurred and were first reported. Finally, all four Gospels are manifestly the work of individuals who proclaim passionately an interpretation of Jesus which was a minority interpretation, and one from this side of the resurrection. While I as an individual share their interpretation—I hope with equal passion—this must not blind me to the difficulties created for the Quest for the historical Jesus via historical research.

Fourth Proposition. The gap between the total reality of an event in history and that which a later historian may make demonstrably probable must be filled by inspiration, intuition, existential encounter, or some other device. In some versions of modern historiography it is contended that for a real encounter with a historical figure it is enough to grasp the basic commitment or intention of that figure. It is that intention which is meaningful in terms of the dialogue between the past and the present. But this does not automatically solve the problem of the gap between the original reality and that which may be made demonstrably probable by a later generation. It is true that this new emphasis permits the historian to encounter a figure out of the past without a full *curriculum vitae,* but it is also true that in some ways it is more difficult to identify the intention of a man than it is to determine a detail of his *curriculum vitae.*

Probably the Gospel writers had no conscious awareness of this gap, but the changes which took place in the tradition were in part an effort to compensate for this loss. The modern scholar who seeks the purely historical Jesus will attempt to remove from the record these compensatory changes; but this merely accentuates the gap between the original reality and that which may be made demonstrably probable. How is this gap to be filled? Perhaps an existential encounter with the historical Jesus is possible through the recovery of his intention—quite apart from the sequence of external facts in his career. But do not the old problems arise even in connection with his "intention"? Exactly what did he mean by the proclamation that the kingdom of God was at hand? (Or should we follow the *New English Bible* which, possibly out of deference to C. H. Dodd translates "the kingdom of God is upon you"?) What did Jesus mean by "Son of man" and how was he related to this concept? To what extent are the passion predictions indicative of Jesus' own understanding of his destiny? (While these predictions occur in all the Synoptics they appear to be derived almost entirely from a single strand of the tradition, namely, that in Mark.)

I recognize that much may still be done toward the resolution of such questions as these. But it remains true that whatever is done the results will be more precarious than Christian faith will find satisfactory.

Fifth Proposition. History cannot *prove* the Gospel or give faith its final validation. One cannot climb the ladder of historical facts to the world of faith. This is true not primarily because of the inadequacy of the historical evidence concerning Jesus of Nazareth, but rather because of the nature of all historical evidence. Ultimate faith, whether Christian, communist, secularist, or some other, involves an affirmation or attitude toward the whole of reality which transcends all possible historical knowledge. It is frequently forgotten that even conclusive evidence for the resurrection of Jesus would not automatically validate the claims made by the Christian community for the significance of that event. If competent medical authorities had declared Jesus to be "dead," and then a few days later equally competent medical authorities had declared him to be alive, this sequence of events might still be regarded as significant medically but meaningless theologically.

If facts cannot prove faith can they disprove it? It is at least plausible to argue that this question should be answered in the affirmative, i.e., "Yes, facts can disprove faith!" Admittedly, since I have argued that all historical knowledge is probability knowledge, it is equally true that any historical knowledge which might disprove the existence of Jesus or prove that he was a basically different person from the one presented in the Gospels would be only a probability knowledge. If such probability knowledge were to appear, those of us who know ourselves to belong to the Christian community could continue to make our Christian affirmations confident that some future discovery would again reverse the tide of probabilities. But when I say that history could disprove faith I mean that *if* it could be established that Jesus never existed, or that he was totally different from what we believe him to have been, then faith *in him* could no longer exist in its present form. However, Christian faith in some other form would probably continue. In other words, Christian faith, as it is commonly understood today, includes not only an affirmation of meaning but also some affirmation of fact.

Certainty about the historicity of the "facts" connected with Jesus' ministry would not of itself produce faith, but certainty about non-historicity of these "facts" would destroy faith or transform it into a different faith.

II

This brings us to the basic problem, namely, the question of the relation between the Jesus of history and the Christ of faith. More precisely formulated, it is the question of the relation between our probability knowledge of the Jesus of history and our religious affirmations concerning the Christ of faith. Central affirmations of the Christian faith such as, "God was in Christ reconciling the world unto himself . . .," or, "The Word became flesh and dwelt among us . . .," such affirmations are obviously and of necessity statements of faith and not of historical knowledge. They transcend the realm of the historical; they cannot be documented in the fashion of ordinary historical events. We are all familiar with this fact and take it for granted in our religious faith. But we would like to imagine that the historical figure who is the center of these theological affirmations is clearly known to us and that the basic historical data concerning him may be known with absolute certainty. But this hope or expectation is frustrated if, as I have argued, all historical knowledge—including historical knowledge of the Bible—is only probability knowledge.

What are the options confronting us as we face this difficulty? A clarification of the logical possibilities open to us may assist in guiding us to our own conclusions.

A first option would be to argue that although historical research in general leads only to probability results the situation with respect to Jesus of Nazareth is in some sense unique and therefore, in this instance, complete historical certainty may be achieved. But this would be tantamount to insisting that the biblical evidence occupies a privileged position as over against other forms of historical evidence or sources. Whatever one's own views may be concerning the Bible it is obviously impossible to ask "historical research" as such to allow a privileged position to historical evidence taken from the biblical tradition. It would be absurd to argue that such and such items had been proved about the Jesus of history if the proof were of such a character that it would not be equally convincing to competent individuals whatever their particular religious or theological views. Furthermore, it has already been argued that an investigation of the Bible demonstrates conclusively that it does not occupy any such privileged position. This is not to deny every possible concept of inspiration, but rather to say that whatever one's concept of inspiration it must be recognized that the presence of an apparently historical statement in a book of the Bible does not guarantee that that historical statement is strictly true in the ordinary sense. It is possible to point out that the considerable diversity in detail in the Gospel records does not obscure a substantial agreement in many matters so far as the evangelists' witness is concerned. But even if this argument is accepted at face value it proves only that there is a higher degree of probability about some items than about others and that the number of items included in this circle of higher probability may be considerably larger than the more skeptical New Testament scholars have been ready to admit. But this leaves the discussion still at the probability level, and it is this "probability" element which creates the problem in connection with the confidence of affirmations of faith.

A second option would be to argue that the risk of faith includes not only the risk of a false interpretation of facts but also the risk of the non-historicity of the alleged facts which the faith seeks to interpret. But surely it is incompatible with the nature of faith that it should be made dependent upon the results of the research carried on by a limited number of highly trained and highly specialized individuals within—or without—the church. Is there not something contrary to the very nature of faith in the suggestion that tomorrow's newspaper could report an archeological discovery or a historical hypothesis that would obliterate the possibility of "looking to Jesus the pioneer and perfecter of our faith" (Heb. 12:2a)? The risk of faith is an intelligible risk when it transcends knowledge and affirms what in the nature of the case can be affirmed only by faith. Does the affirmation, "Jesus is Lord!" mean anything at all when it is paraphrased, "Jesus is Lord, i.e., he is Lord unless the latest discoveries have proved that he did not exist or that he was totally other than that which we assume him to have been." The question answers itself. We know that the affirmation "Jesus is Lord" can, at least theoretically, be refuted by eternity; but it is surely not an affirmation which can be refuted by an accidental, archaeological discovery (or a historical hypothesis). But is this the risk that is inherent in the distinctive character of historical religion? I think not. Historical religion is religion in which the encounter with God occurs through historical happenings. But this statement does not answer the question of the precise relation between the historical happenings and the encounter. It could be—as will be suggested in the next option—that the kerygma, though triggered by historical events, transcends them so as to be independent of the details of those events and therefore independent of any conceivable discoveries by historical research. For the moment I am content to argue that faith which is dependent on the latest archaeological bulletin cannot be faith, and that the idea of historical religion does not of itself require any such impossible position.

The third option, already suggested, is that the kerygma, though born in history, rises above its origin so as to be independent of it. Against such a view it has been argued that this would be a docetic version of the Christian faith and that it would transform Christianity into a religion based on the myth or idea of victory over sin and death rather than a religion based on an actual

victory made real in the life of a historical person, Jesus of Nazareth. This cannot mean that if movie camera and tape recorder
had been present during the ministry of Jesus the events they
would have recorded would have demanded with absolute necessity the language of faith, "The Word became flesh . . ." or "God
was in Christ. . . ." But it does mean, so it is argued, that the
events which would have been recorded by this hypothetical tape
recorder and movie camera would have been consistent with such
statements.

In the third century the charge of docetism would have been a
serious charge, and no doubt it still is today. But it should be remembered that the option suggested here does not deny that God
worked in and through flesh-and-blood history. What it denies is
that the kerygma which emerged through that history can be so
identified with it that research into the history can be definitive
for the kerygma itself. Undoubtedly there are difficulties in this
option, but I suspect that it deserves more serious consideration
than it has received in some quarters. Obviously this view will be
unsatisfactory both to those who regard Jesus primarily as an example and to those who hold that what he did produced of itself
an objective change in the relation of God to the world of men.
But this shift of the focus from the historical figure to the revelation or kerygma that came into the world through him is possible
for those who hold that the message which emerged is God's instrument in transforming our relation to him.

Yet, while I am prepared to speak in defense of this option
which separates the Christ of faith from the Jesus of history, I
must confess that it does not satisfy me because it does not do
justice to the actual experience of faith. The actual experience of
faith, insofar as I am able to analyze it, is a response to the Christ
proclaimed in the Gospels. But this response includes the certainty that this Christ is, in the deepest sense, a continuation of
the Jesus who walked in Galilee. In this *fourth option* one argues
from faith to history, or, to put it more precisely, the affirmation

of faith includes an affirmation concerning history, the history of Jesus of Nazareth.

III

There are some serious objections to this option. So let me explain why I favor it, what it does *not* mean, and what it does mean.

From the perspective of historical research it is a theoretical possibility that the Jesus of history never existed or that he was totally different from the Jesus proclaimed in the Gospels. As a New Testament historian I am fully aware of this theoretical possibility, even though the objective evidence currently available makes it an unlikely possibility. Yet if I really believed that tomorrow's paper could bring news of an archaeological discovery disproving the existence of Jesus I should await the morning newspaper with a "fear and trembling" very different from that described by Kierkegaard. But I do not wait in such "fear and trembling." I *know* that future archaeological discoveries are not going to produce such evidence. I can only conclude that this basic confidence is given in the Christian experience itself. As Christian I am saying "Yes" to the living Word that is proclaimed to me through the Scriptures, through the preaching, or through some other aspect of the life of the Christian community. But in saying "Yes" to this living Word I am also saying "Yes" to the witness of the community that this Word was not plucked capriciously or cleverly out of the air but that it was the Word lived and proclaimed in Jesus of Nazareth—that the Word became flesh before it became kerygma. My affirmation of faith includes an affirmation about history—an affirmation about a particular bit of history that happened in Palestine around A.D. 30.

However, I do not wish to exaggerate what is claimed to be known about history through the affirmation of faith. First of all, I am not claiming that this "evidence" of faith can be used by the secular historian to establish the historicity or the character of

Jesus. The secular historian must proceed about his business in the usual way. In fact, as a New Testament historian I proceed with him along that same road of historical research. But in a very profound sense I have inside information. I repeat, I have inside information. I do not know what surprising turns the road may take before the end is reached, but I know something about what, or who, would be found at the end of the road if historical research were able to follow that road to the very end. Since this "evidence" cannot be used like an ordinary piece of evidence in historical research, it will have to be called subjective evidence as over against objective evidence—if this type of distinction is of assistance. But remember that the question with which I am dealing is not how to convince the scholars of the world that there is an identity between the Christ of faith and the Jesus of history, but rather how the man of faith is to relate his affirmations of faith to the probability results of historical research. And for this concern of the man of faith it is not necessary that his evidence be convincing to those who stand outside the circle of faith.

Furthermore, I do not claim that it is possible to argue from faith to the historicity of particular items in the Gospel tradition, e.g., Peter's confession, the baptism of Jesus, or the triumphal entry. Particular stories may be entirely apocryphal and yet witness accurately to the quality, character, or significance of the person about whom they are related. I have repeatedly told my students that if it were possible to classify all the stories about Lincoln as either "true" or "apocryphal," it would then be possible to create a valid portrait of him using only the "apocryphal" materials. So it is with the stories about Jesus. It is unnecessary and impossible to argue from the affirmations of faith to the *details* of his life and ministry. What is necessary is confidence in an essential continuity and commensurability between the Gospel portrait and the Jesus of history.

Before commenting further on "continuity and commensurability" it may be helpful to say a word about discontinuity. The

Gospel tradition developed in a believing community which stood on this side of Good Friday and Easter. The faith of the disciples after the resurrection was different from their faith before that event, and their understanding of Jesus was correspondingly different. Thus there was a degree of discontinuity between the disciples' understanding of Jesus before and after Easter. This is true even if one assumes that Peter's confession at Caesarea Philippi (Mark 8:27–29, and parallels) is essentially historical and not a post-Easter confession projected back into the ministry. It is difficult to state with certainty how great this discontinuity was. Since the ways of God are not the ways of men it may have been even greater than we would have expected. It must be remembered that in the first century many who expected the Messiah did not recognize him in Jesus because they believed too confidently that they knew in advance what manner of person he would be. In a sense we are confronted with the reverse problem. From the pages of the New Testament we know the Christ of faith, and he has been confirmed in the life of the Christian community. But we must not argue back too confidently from this Christ to the ministry of Jesus, as if we knew exactly what manner of man he must have been. God is a God of surprises. He uses "even things that are not, to bring to nothing things that are . . ." (I Cor. 1:28b). There is a real continuity and commensurability between the Jesus of the ministry and the resurrected Christ, but the resurrection did involve a transformation. Easter was not simply another day. It made a difference. It created a degree of discontinuity.

What this fourth option asserts, then, is that despite discontinuity the affirmation of faith in response to the Christ of the Gospels includes the confidence that there is an essential continuity and commensurability between this Christ and the Jesus of the ministry. Continuity means that the portrait in the Gospels is really based on Jesus of Nazareth and not on some other person, or on no person at all; commensurability means that there is an essential correspondence between the earthly Jesus and the Gospel portrait, i.e., a correspondence in the quality, intention, and thrust of the life. When the total history is unveiled here or hereafter—more likely hereafter!—we may be astonished at the unexpected ways in which the continuity and commensurability actually existed. But they will be there.

When it is contended that one cannot argue from faith to fact, that this is a violation of basic methodological principles, I can reply only that the Christian does actually argue in this fashion. It may also be added, in defense of this form of argument, that in other areas of life something at least analogous occurs. Even in our American culture there is many a husband who if asked whether he were certain of his wife's faithfulness would reply with an unhesitating affirmative. If he were asked whether he meant that he was ninety-five percent certain or even ninety-nine percent certain, he might well be indignant at this suggestion of the possibility of doubt. Such a husband could be perfectly well aware of the theoretical possibility of his wife's unfaithfulness. He might even have read the Kinsey reports and have seen other statistics on the fickleness of women. But these theoretical possibilities do not affect his confidence in his wife, a confidence which is based not on statistical probabilities or historical research but on the faith arising out of his encounter with his wife. From this faith he argues to the realm of fact concerning her conduct. All analogies have their limitations, and they do not prove but only illustrate. But in some such sense it is possible and even inevitable that the Christian, normally quite unconsciously, argues from faith to fact. When the encounter with the Gospel of the Christ produces conviction, this conviction includes the confidence that the portrait is not of a dream but of a historical reality. I do not see that the confidence which Christians feel about the Jesus of history can be explained in any other way. Certainly this confidence goes far beyond the relative certainty which may be provided by historical research.

Perhaps a second analogy may serve to bring out the concepts of continuity and commensurability. A man walks on a cliff overlooking a lake. He turns toward the lake to see below him a great splash. He knows immediately, simply by looking at the splash, that a large stone or similar object has been thrown into the lake. If he is an amateur physicist he knows that there is a relation between the nature of the splash and the weight, size, shape, and velocity of the object creating it. There is a commensurability between the splash and the stone; there is also a continuity in the sense that the splash occurs only when and where the stone strikes the water. The analogy may appear ludicrous or awkward, but for the present purpose it is obvious that the stone equals the historical Jesus while the splash corresponds with the Gospel portrait. So the man who responds in faith to the Gospel portrait knows that there is a continuity and commensurability between that portrait and the historical Jesus. This certainty, however, will not enable him to write a "Life" of Jesus or even to choose between the differing "Lives" proferred him by scholars. For example, it will not enable him to choose between the sketches of Jesus presented by Bornkamm and Stauffer.

At first glance it might seem that this analogy, insofar as it is valid, eliminates the necessity for faith. After all, it does not require a special affirmation of faith for an observer to move from the splash to the stone or other object behind the splash. But faith enters in in connection with the evaluation of the splash, and not as the link between splash and stone. Two men read the Gospel records. One sees, or experiences, the splash and from his response knows that it partakes of reality and is not merely a literary creation or phantasy. Because of this sense of the reality of the splash he knows, when he pauses to analyze the matter, that there was a continuity and commensurability between the object and the splash created. The other reader sees only the *description* of a splash and not a splash which he himself experiences as a part of reality. Since the description of a splash has no necessary relation to actuality and may be a purely literary product, this reader has no compulsion to reason back from the alleged splash to an actual object occasioning it. But where the Gospel portrait becomes a reality through which a man knows that his life has been "grasped," the reality of the figure behind the portrait is necessarily given, even though the details of that figure cannot be determined from this experience.

In this connection it may be fruitful to digress for a comment on the views which have been expressed by the distinguished New Testament scholar, Professor John Knox. Probably no American scholar has dealt more carefully with the problem which concerns us here than has Professor Knox in various of his writings. His general position was established in the trilogy now conveniently published in the single volume *Jesus: Lord and Christ.*[4] He contends that while the details of the historical life may be uncertain the Christian community is unquestionably and indisputably the result of that life. The Christian, who participates in the continuing life of this community, affirms that the emergence of this community was the act of God. This is an affirmation of faith and cannot be demonstrated by the traditional techniques of the historian or the scientist. But the historical reality about which this affirmation is made, i.e., the Christian community, is unquestionably a historical reality, and no acids of historical research will ever destroy this fact. Up to this point the view of Professor Knox is basically parallel to that espoused by Bultmann. Both men shift the focus of historical certainty from the ministry of Jesus to that which resulted from the ministry. Bultmann speaks of the kerygma which resulted, while Knox prefers to stress the church, i.e., the community which proclaimed and responded to that kerygma. This is an important difference between the two, but thus far their basic methodologies would seem to be parallel.

However, in a more recent study, *The Church and the Reality*

---

[4] New York: Harper, 1958.

of Christ,[5] Professor Knox seeks to go beyond the conclusions already established.[6] Now he insists that the Christian affirms something about the historical happenings which preceded the emergence of the church. "It belongs to our existence as Christians to affirm the actuality of Jesus' existence—and not merely the bare fact of it, but something of the full distinctive quality of it" (p. 21). How is this possible in view of the uncertainties which beset the conclusions derived from historical research? Knox is fully aware of these uncertainties of historical research, but in this book—and particularly in the chapter entitled "The Church and Its Memory"—he argues that in addition to the knowledge derived from the New Testament the church carries in its *memory* a genuine knowledge of the historical Jesus. This knowledge does not include dates and details but, rather, a grasp of the quality and character of the person. Knox points out that "the image of Jesus himself which the Church carries in its heart cannot be derived simply and solely from the Gospels and has not in fact been derived from that source" (p. 52). This image has been derived in part from the memory of the community, a memory in which all its members participate. The seriousness with which Knox takes this concept of memory is indicated by his willingness to identify certain elements in this memory which go beyond the evidence provided—however ambiguously—in the Gospels. Two such items are suggested. Thus, according to Knox, the Christian community knows through its memory of Jesus that his "personal moral stature" was even greater than the Gospels alone demonstrate. In similar fashion it knows that there was an agape-character to the intimate relationship between Jesus and his disciples which is not fully presented in the Gospels.

If this striking hypothesis is correct, then the memory of the Christian community serves both to validate the continuity and

---

[5] New York: Harper, 1962.
[6] This further step may have been implicit in his earlier writings but it certainly was not in the foreground of his presentation.

commensurability between the Gospel portrait and the historical Jesus and to add certain touches to that portrait.

Professor Knox has analyzed the power and function of memory with great persuasiveness. Before accepting his position as a whole, however, my own skepticism would need to be assuaged on at least two points.

First, is it really possible to argue that the Christian community today possesses a knowledge of the historical Jesus which is derived from *memory* as distinct from the traditions preserved in the New Testament or ancillary documents? The examples used by Professor Knox illustrate vividly how memory may serve as a link between the first and the third generation. But can one argue that it fulfills this function after sixty generations? To put it differently, is the image of Christ in the church today derived in any significant sense from memory, or is it derived entirely from the portrait in the New Testament and reflection on that portrait? Suppose we were to discover an isolated Christian community which had come into existence in response to a stray copy of the New Testament, a community which had never had any other contact with the church at large. Would this Christian community, born out of the reading of the New Testament, be deficient in its image of Christ when compared with other Christian communities which have participated in the chain of memory outside the New Testament.[7] Admittedly the image in the heart of the church may differ slightly from the portrait objectively present in the New Testament. But is the explanation of this difference to be found by an appeal to the effective memory of the church, or is it rather the result of the play of devout or popular imagination on the New Testament portrait?

Second, even if it were granted that the church retains a strand of memory of the historical Jesus which is independent of the New Testament, could this strand of memory be regarded as re-

[7] Admittedly the theological formulations which they had developed might differ from those of the church generally, but that is another matter.

liable? After all, the New Testament itself is a cross section of the church's memory, but from the second or third generation of that memory. If historical certainty cannot be derived from this cross section of early memory, how is it possible to argue that a strand of sixtieth-generation memory may provide that certainty?

A further perplexity is created by this hypothesis when one asks concerning its relation to affirmations based on historical research and affirmations based on deductions arising out of the faith encounter itself. I have assumed that affirmations about historical reality were of necessity derived either from historical research, taking that term in the broadest possible sense, or from the experience of faith in one form or another. But in which of these two categories is the *memory* of the church to be placed? Professor Knox is apparently insistent that it is impossible to argue from affirmations of faith to affirmations about history.[8] Therefore it may be presumed that he does not regard "memory" as falling in that category. On the other hand, he states quite explicitly that the data provided by memory will not be acceptable as evidence to the ordinary, secular historian.[9] But what is this *tertium quid* category which is not acceptable to the historian as historian nor is it the distinctive faith territory of the Christian as Christian? Perhaps Knox would agree that this memory is a part of the distinctive experience of the Christian as Christian, though he is eager to demonstrate that it is not a deduction from faith as I have assumed distinctive Christian knowledge must be.

The questions suggested here will need to be discussed from various angles before there can be a final evaluation of the thesis advocated by Professor Knox. However, it should be noted that his view shares with the position taken here the conviction that the affirmations of Christian faith include affirmations about the

---

[8] See *The Church and the Reality of Christ,* pp. 80 f.
[9] *Ibid.,* p. 57.

historical Jesus.[10] So far as I am able to analyze the structure of Christian faith and the structure of my own faith it includes—consciously or unconsciously—a confidence in the continuity and commensurability of the Jesus of history with the Christ of faith. We know that he really existed and that he was not Judas or Barabbas! While historical research may provide visible props for this confidence, faith is not finally dependent upon them. The discovery of the ultimate reality in the Gospel portrait includes assurance concerning the historical reality of the figure behind that portrait.

It should be clear that I am not attempting to discover a historical Jesus who will then serve as a norm or control by which to evaluate the Christ of faith proclaimed in the Gospels. The kerygma came through the history. It was heard by the community of those who participated in that particular piece of history. The New Testament witnesses to what those in that community heard God saying to them through that experience. It is not possible for us to recapture the historical experience through which they passed and then to sit in judgment on the kerygma which they proclaimed. The effort which began in the eighteenth century to get behind the Christ of faith can never produce a norm by which the Christ of faith may be judged, since the norm is not the Jesus of history *in himself* but that which God said and did through him. The Word became "flesh" that it might be lived out in the midst of our historical existence. But it is the Word and not the flesh which brings life. A knowledge of the historical Jesus, like a knowledge of the particular situations in which the New Testament writings were produced, assists in understanding what was and is being said through the kerygma. But it does not provide some objective point of reference with which to judge what God intended through that Jesus of history.

Having spoken of the affirmations of faith let me add a post-

[10] Cf. the statement we have already quoted from him:". . . the image of Jesus himself which the Church carries in its heart cannot be derived simply and solely from the Gospels and has not in fact been derived from that source" (*ibid.*, p. 52).

script about doubt. Most of us have experienced it. It has been argued that it is an inevitable and perhaps necessary concomitant of faith. I suspect that when doubt becomes dominant it is not really doubt about the actuality of Jesus but rather doubt arising because we no longer respond to, or are grasped by, the Word of God that was "manifested in the flesh" and "preached among the nations" (I Tim. 3:16). When this link with the eternal Word fails, we, the children of an age obsessed with historical facts, defend ourselves by saying we can no longer believe in this or that historical fact traditionally associated with the ministry of Jesus. But the real problem of faith and doubt moves at a far deeper level. When the Word still speaks to our lives we are not troubled by uncertainties concerning the flesh in which it was incarnate. We know that whatever the details of that life may have been it was continuous and commensurable with the Christ who has spoken to us through the Gospels. "Blessed are those who have not seen and yet believe."

Appendix

A LIST OF SIXTEENTH-CENTURY GOSPEL HARMONIES

The information given for each of the harmonies listed below was supplied from my notes, compiled on a sabbatical leave in Europe in 1961–62. At the time, bibliographical requirements were not uppermost in my mind, and my notes are accordingly incomplete in places. Since the bibliographies against which they could be checked are often scanty and inaccurate, I have not been able to verify the notes in every instance or to supply some of the missing data.

The harmonies are listed in chronological order; the date given is the date of the first edition. Following the publication facts, it is noted whether the editor was Protestant or Catholic and in what language(s) the first edition was printed. Each harmony is then characterized as *integrated* (as in Tatian's *Diatessaron*), or *parallel* (as in most modern harmonies and synopses), or *horizontal, parallel* (where the parallels from the various Gospels are quoted *ad seriatim*). Any additional comments are given next.

The libraries where copies of the harmonies are available are referred to as follows:

Augsburg—The Staats- und Stadtbibliothek

Edinburgh—The University of Edinburgh

Freiburg—The University of Freiburg

Hartford—The Hartford Seminary Foundation

Harvard—Harvard University

Heidelberg—The University of Heidelberg

London—The British Museum

Munich—The Staatsbibliothek

New York—Union Theological Seminary
Paris—Bibliothèque Nationale
Tübingen—The University of Tübingen
Yale—Yale University

MICHAEL MEMLER. *Quatuor Evangeliorum Consonantia.* Mainz, 1524. Catholic. Latin; integrated. Chiefly a repetition of Victor of Capua's Latin version of Tatian. Copies available in Paris, Yale (1532 ed.).

OTHMAR NACHTGALL (LUSCINIUS). *Evangelicae Historiae . . . Domini Jesu Christi . . .* Erfurt, 1524. Catholic. Latin, German; integrated. Based on Victor of Capua's Latin version of Tatian. Copies available in London (1525 German ed.), Augsburg (1525 German ed.), Yale (1525 German ed.).

MARTIN BUCER. *Enarrationum in Evangelia Matthaei, Marci, et Lucae. Libri Duo.* Strassburg, 1527. Protestant. Latin. The work is primarily a commentary; in discussing Matthew, however, Bucer also considered those passages from Mark and Luke which he regarded as parallels. In the subsequent section he considered the material from Mark and Luke not already discussed. The 1530 edition included the Gospel of John. The work was important because it influenced Calvin, who followed Bucer's rather free handling of the materials as over against the rigidities of Osiander. Copy available in Freiburg.

ROBERT GOULLET (GOULETUS). *Tetramonon Evangeliorum.* Paris, 1535. Catholic. Latin; horizontal, parallel. For reference purposes the chapters of the Gospels are numbered and then subdivided into sections marked A, B, C, etc. In general, the order of the Gospel of John is followed. Copies available in Freiburg, Paris.

ANDREAS OSIANDER. *Harmoniae Evangelicae.* Basel, 1537. Protestant. Latin, Greek. The harmony was integrated but employed an elaborate system of letters to indicate the relationship of the materials quoted to the various Gospels. It also contained a lengthy *Elenchus Harmoniae Evangelicae* which summarized the Gospels in four vertical columns. The work was noteworthy because of Osiander's insistence that the order of each Gospel should be regarded as strictly historical. Copies available in Tübingen, London, Paris, Yale (1545 ed.).

ANTONIUS BROICKIUS OF KÖNIGSTEIN. *Enarratio in Monotessaron* (sometimes entitled *In Quatuor Evangelia Enarrationum*). Cologne, 1539. Catholic. Latin; generally integrated, but occasionally horizontal, parallel. Part I deals with the Synoptics up to the passion narrative (plus a few Johannine passages); Part II deals with the rest of John and with the passion narrative in all four Gospels. Copies available in Freiburg, London, Paris, Yale (1542 ed.).

F. GABRIEL À PUTEO. *Tetramonon sive Symphonia et Concentus Quatuor Evangeliorum.* Paris, 1547. Catholic. Latin; integrated, but with lettering system to indicate use of Gospels. Copy available in Freiburg.

CORNELIUS JANSEN. *Concordia Evangelica.* Louvain, 1549. Catholic. Latin; integrated. Jansen apparently borrowed his system of symbols from Osiander, or else both used some earlier source. Tends to follow John's order. Copies available in Heidelberg, Tübingen, Paris (1558 ed.), London (1596 ed.), New York (1613 ed.).

JOACHIM PERION. *Gestis Jesu Christi . . . ex Quatuor . . . Monotessaron.* Paris, 1553. Catholic. Latin; integrated. Really a loose paraphrase of the Gospel narrative, somewhat carelessly put together. Copies available in Freiburg, Paris, London.

ALOYS MIRÉ. *La Concordance des quatre Évangélistes* (1561 ed.). Paris, 1553. Catholic. French; integrated but with a complicated system of letters to indicate sources (the Gospels, Acts, I Cor.). Copies available in Paris (1561 ed.), London (1562 ed.).

GUTERRIUS DE TREJO. *In Sacrasancta Jesu Christi Quattuor Evangelia.* Seville, 1554. Catholic. Latin; integrated. Copies available in London, Paris.

JOHN CALVIN. *Harmonia ex Tribus Evangelistis Composita.* Geneva, 1555. Protestant. Latin; parallel. A commentary on a harmony of the Synoptic Gospels. Calvin exercised considerable freedom in rearranging the sequence of the narratives. In general he appears to have followed the order of Matthew, though this was probably a matter of convenience rather than conviction. Contains verse as well as chapter references. Copies available in Edinburgh, London, Paris (1563 ed.), New York (1560 ed.), Yale (1582 ed.), Hartford (1582 ed.).

NATALINO AMULIO OF PADUA. *Adunatione dei quattro Evangelisti.* Venice, 1556. Catholic. Italian; integrated. Copy available in London.

MATTHIAS FLACIUS ILLYRICUS. *Ecclesiastica Historia.* Basel, 1559. Protestant. Latin; strictly speaking, not a harmony but an integrated paraphrase of the Gospels. Copies available in Heidelberg, Paris, Harvard (ed. of 1560 ff.), London (ed. of 1561 ff.), Yale (ed. of 1562 ff.), Hartford (1574 ed.).

REINHARD LUTZ. *Harmonia, seu Historia Sancta Omnium quae Verissima, de Christo.* Basel, 1561. Protestant. Latin; integrated in a rather haphazard fashion. Parallels sometimes given simply as a reference, i.e., without actual quotation. Copies available in Freiburg, Paris, New York.

LAURENTIUS CODOMANN (CODMAN). *Harmonia Evangelistarum.* Nuremberg, 1568. Protestant. German; integrated but with extensive lettering system to indicate use of Gospels. Clearly of the "Osiander" type. Copy available in Tübingen.

CHARLES DU MOULIN (CAROLUS MOLINAEUS). *Collatio et Unio Quatuor Evangelistarum Domini Nostri Jesu Christi.* Paris, 1565. Protestant; parallel. Even more rigid than Osiander in retaining each Gospel in its own order. Copies available in London, Paris.

PAUL CRELL. *Evangelion unsers Herrn Jesu Christi . . . aus allen vier Evangelisten . . .* (1571). Wittenberg, 1566. Protestant. German and Latin; parallel. A limited edition in German and Latin, intended for the nobility, appeared in 1566. The German edition for general circulation appeared in 1571. Crell indicates that vertical, parallel columns were now recognized as the best method for preparing a harmony. He also states that he was continuing the work begun by his teacher Johann Bugenhagen. Copy available in London.

JEAN DU BUISSON (JOANNES BUISONIUS). *Historia et Harmonia Evangelica.* Douay, 1571. Catholic. Latin; chiefly integrated, but with some characteristics of the parallel harmony inasmuch as parallel passages from the Gospels are sometimes quoted in italics in the margin. John's order is closely followed; apparently that of Mark is also. Copies available in Paris, Yale (1575 ed.).

JOANNES M. VERRATUS OF FERRARA. *Harmonia Evangelica.* Venice, 1571. Catholic. Latin.

ALAN COPE (COPUS). *Syntaxis Historiae Evangelicae.* Louvain, 1572. Catholic. Latin; parallel. John's order is generally followed, as is that of Matthew. Copies available in Heidelberg, London, Paris.

CHRISTOPHER FISCHER. *Harmonia Evangelistarum.* Lüneberg, 1575. Protestant. German. A series of sermons based on a harmony of the Gospel texts. Copy of Volume I available in Augsburg.

THOMAS BEAUX-AMIS. *Commentariorum in Evangelicam Harmoniam.* Paris, 1583 ff. Catholic. Latin; parallel. A voluminous commentary; it is not clear whether the fourth and final volume ever appeared. Copies available in London, Heidelberg (ed. of 1594 ff.).

ALPHONSUS SALMERON. *Commentarii in Evangelicam Historiam.* Madrid, 1585 ff. Catholic. Latin. Not a true harmony, the material being arranged by topics (e.g., Book VI is entitled "Miracles," Book VII, "Parables"); within these divisions, however, there are many comments on the problem of harmonization. Copies available in Heidelberg, New York (ed. of 1612 ff.), Yale (ed. of 1602 ff.), Harvard (ed. of 1612 ff.).

GEORGE STEINHARD. *Evangelistarium.* Leipzig, 1588. Protestant. German. Copy available in Munich.

CESARE BARONIO (BARONIUS). *Annales Ecclesiastici.* Rome, 1589. Catholic. Latin; integrated. Not strictly a harmony, but a two-hundred page resume of the life of Jesus from birth to resurrection. Gives special praise to harmony of Cornelius Jansen. Copies available in Freiburg, Yale (ed. of 1602 ff.), New York (1614 ed.), Harvard (1623 ed.), Hartford (1641 ed.).

HEINRICH BÜNTING. *Harmonia Evangelistarum.* Magdeburg, 1589. Protestant; integrated. Detailed dating of events in

Jesus' ministry by years, months, and days. Copy available in Munich.

MARTIN CHEMNITZ. *Harmonia Quatuor Evangelistarum.* Frankfurt, 1593 ff. Protestant. Greek and Latin; integrated, but combined with vertical or horizontal parallels (the editions vary). The original edition was completed and published posthumously; many editions appeared. Copies available in London (ed. of 1608 ff.), Yale (1628 ed.), New York (1641 ed.), Heidelberg (1645 ed.), Hartford (1704 ed.).

GERHARD MERCATOR. *Evangelicae Historiae Quadripartitae Monas.* Duisburg, 1592 (1569). Protestant (see chapter four *supra*). Latin; parallel. In his *Chronologia* of 1569, Mercator included a harmony of the four Gospels arranged in four vertical columns; however, for the sake of brevity the Gospel narratives were generally not quoted *in toto* but merely indicated by the quotation of the opening and closing lines. At the very end of his life Mercator returned to the problem of harmonization and produced a full-scale harmony, which was published in 1592. In general he followed the "Osiander" pattern. Copies available in Heidelberg, London, Paris.

MATTHIEU DU CHATEAU (MATTHAEUS À CASTRO). *Epitome Concordiae Jansenianae.* Antwerp, 1593. Catholic. Latin; integrated. Chiefly Jansen's harmony, with comments added. Copy available in Paris.

SEBASTIAN BARRADAS. *Commentaria in Evangelicam Historiam.* Venice, 1599. Catholic. Latin; integrated. Not strictly a harmony; presented the life of Jesus in detail, arranged in the sequence Barradas regarded as historical. Copies available in Heidelberg, Paris (1601 ed.).

BARTHOLOMEW SCULTETUS. *Diarium Humanitatis Domini Nostri*

Jesu Christi. Frankfurt, 1600. Protestant. German; integrated. Leans toward the "Osiander" pattern but is not as strict. Dates the events in Jesus' ministry, giving years, months, and sometimes days. Copy available in New York.

Additional Titles

The following titles have not been included in the foregoing list since my information on them is so scanty. It should be noted that in neither of these lists have I included harmonies of the passion narratives, which were popular in the sixteenth century.

G. L. *Christi ab Incarnationis usque Ascensionis Gesta.* 1514.

COMPILER? *Die vier Evangelia in ainer formlichen Ordnung mit allen Cancordantzen.* 1527.

G. DE BRANTEGHEM. *Jesu Christi Vita, juxta Quatuor Evangelistarum Narrationes.* 1537.

SIMON CORROY. *Consonantia Evangelica.* 1547.

BENJAMIN BEAUPORT. *Harmoniae suae Expositio.* 1552.

DIDACUS VILLALOBOS. *Concordia.* 1555.

PETER DE IRUROSQUI. *Evangelii.* 1557.

JOHN MATHESIUS. *Historia Jesu Christi.* 1568.

MICHAEL FOUQUE. Title? 1574.

G. SIGELIUS. *Synopsis Historiae Jesu Christi.* 1583.

JOANNES AVENARIUS. *Harmonia Evangelica.* 1583.

Body, 11 on 13 and 10 on 11 Garamond
Display, Garamond
Paper, University (Warren) Text

Index

INDEX OF SCRIPTURE PASSAGES

NAME AND SUBJECT INDEX

Type, 11 on 13 and 10 on 11 Garamond
Display, Garamond
Paper, University (Warren's Text)